ENGAGING
PARENTS AS ALLIES

Y★UTH MINISTRY IN THE TRENCHES

ENGAGING

PARENTS AS ALLIES

Y★UTH MINISTRY IN THE TRENCHES

Wayne Rice

Standard®
PUBLISHING
Bringing The Word to Life

Cincinnati, Ohio

Published by Standard Publishing, Cincinnati, Ohio
www.standardpub.com

Also available from the Youth Ministry in the Trenches series: *Building & Mobilizing
Teams* and *Reaching Unchurched Teens*

Printed in the United States of America

Project editor: Robert Irvin

Cover and interior design: Thinkpen Design, Inc., www.thinkpendesign.com

Series contributor: David Olshine

ISBN 978-0-7847-2317-3

Library of Congress Cataloging-in-Publication Data

Rice, Wayne.
  Engaging parents as allies / Wayne Rice.
     p. cm. -- (Youth ministry in the trenches series)
  ISBN 978-0-7847-2317-3 (perfect bound)
  1. Church work with youth. 2. Parent and teenager--Religious
aspects--Christianity. I. Title.
  BV4447.R439 2009
  259'.23--dc22
                                    2009011122

15 14 13 12 11 10 09   9 8 7 6 5 4 3 2 1

CONTENTS

WHY OUR THINKING MUST CHANGE

I t was in the early 1980s that I began paying attention to the research being done on the spiritual growth of teenagers. As a career youth worker and cofounder of an organization dedicated to providing resources and training for youth workers (Youth Specialties), I was hoping that at least one of those studies would confirm that youth workers in the church ranked right up there with parents—maybe even outranked them!—as the primary influencers of religious faith in teenagers.

Almost thirty years have passed and many more studies have been done on this topic. But not one of them has elevated youth workers to a place of prominence that is equal with parents on the coveted list of "most important influences" in a teenager's spiritual life. What they have found, however, and continue to find, is that teenagers with a strong religious faith and a strong connection to the church more often than not have parents with a strong religious faith and a strong connection to the church as well. In other words, it's all about the parents.

Once I started buying into what the research was really saying—which was about the same time my own children became teenagers—I decided to do something about it. First, I started paying a lot more attention to my own kids. Second, I enlisted some parenting experts and youth workers to help me create a seminar for parents of teens and preteens; we called it Understanding Your Teenager. And for more than twenty years now I've been trying to help parents stay connected with their kids so they can leverage the immense amount of influence they have simply because they *are* parents. I still believe in youth ministry, but I've been convinced for a long time now that the most important thing a youth worker can do is encourage and equip parents to do what only they can do.

This isn't the first book on parent ministry; it won't be the last. It's exciting to see that ministry to, and through, parents is finally getting some much-needed traction, not only in youth ministry circles but also in the church at large. More and more voices in and around ministry circles are calling for the church to find new ways to make the home the primary place were faith is sown and grown in the lives of children and teens. My hope is that this book will help a great deal with that movement.

TRUTH FROM THE TRENCHES

A credible study hasn't been completed yet that places youth workers in a place of prominence equal with parents on the coveted list of "most important influences" in a teenager's spiritual life.

Acknowledgments, dedication

I'm indebted to a number of friends and colleagues who have written or taught on this subject in recent years and influenced my thinking. I admit I've stolen more than a few good ideas from them. Special thanks to Mark DeVries, Marv Penner, Jim Burns, Dave Lynn, Walt Mueller, Rich Van Pelt, and many others. Thanks also to David Olshine for suggesting this book to the good folks at Standard Publishing.

This book is dedicated, with gratitude, to Jim and Daryl, Joe and Debbie, Mary and Gary . . . great parents and family members who have been a great encouragement to me.

Wayne Rice   LAKESIDE, CALIFORNIA

PART ONE

THINKING IT THROUGH

THINKING ABOUT YOUTH MINISTRY

grew up in the dark ages of youth ministry. There weren't too many churches with youth pastors or youth programs or even youth groups when I was a teenager. If there were activities for "the young people of the church" they were more often than not planned by parents, volunteers, or the teens themselves. Fifty years ago youth ministry was still in its infancy.

My first youth group experience was not in church but in a Youth for Christ (YFC) Bible Club that met after the final bell at my high school. Every Tuesday, an old, yellow, smoke-belching church bus with "Jesus is the Way the Truth and the Life!" printed in big letters on the side would pull up in front of the school right after classes were over, the driver blaring the bus horn. Everybody in the school knew it was time for YFC Bible Club!

Even though I was a Christian I avoided getting on that church bus for two and a half years. There was no way I was going to get on that bus in full view of my friends at school. But during my junior year, my father asked if I knew about the YFC Club that met at my school. He learned about it from some businessmen friends of his and thought I should check it out. I pled for mercy—but Dad insisted I go.

I finally got up the courage to sneak on that old yellow bus one Tuesday afternoon; I desperately hoped that none of my friends would notice. I was surprised to discover that not all of the students who attended this club were losers. In fact there were a couple of guys who played on the varsity basketball team and several girls who were very popular on campus.

The YFC club director was a young guy named Sam. He had a big grin, played the guitar, and told funny jokes. When he taught his Bible lessons, he didn't sound anything like the preachers I was used to hearing. I thought he was very cool.

The following year I became the president of that YFC club and, while in college, joined the YFC staff; I took Sam's job when he moved on. In many ways I ended up becoming a lot like Sam. I learned to play guitar and tell jokes and give interesting Bible talks just like Sam did. He was a huge influence in my life and I've told him so more than once. But he's always shrugged it off and humbly pointed to the fact that I was raised in a Christian home. "I didn't influence you nearly as much as your mom and dad did," he always says. "Thank them, not me."

While I'm still grateful for Sam's example, I know he's right. While my parents never had any ministry training—dad was a building contractor and mom was a . . . mom—I know they taught me life's most important lessons and modeled for me what it means to serve Christ. There's no question that my parents had more influence on my life than anyone else.

A FEW YEARS LATER

Four decades have passed and I'm still involved in youth ministry. Over the years I've worked with hundreds of students in dozens of churches and parachurch ministries. I'm sorry to say that I haven't done a very good job of keeping track of all the students I've known over the years, but once in a while I do hear from one of them. Most are middle-aged adults by now, have become parents of teenagers themselves, and some even have grandchildren (which seems impossible, but it's true).

Let me tell you about Doug Haag, a former student of mine who became the youth pastor at a large church in Southern California. Doug called me one night after a dinner was held in his honor celebrating his twenty-five years of ministry at his church. He was thinking about me, he said, and just wanted to call and say thanks for inspiring him as a high school student so many years ago. I must admit I was feeling a good deal of pride as Doug described my ministry in glowing terms, showering me with praise.

But while I was taking it all in, God was also whispering in my ear. "Wayne . . . before your head swells up too big, keep in mind that Doug's mother and father were missionaries in Mexico, a godly couple who kept Christ at the center of their home and family life. And surely you remember how supportive Doug's parents were of your involvement in his life. And surely you remember how much Doug loved his mom and dad and how proud he was of the work they were doing in Mexico. Do you really think *you* are the reason Doug has been such a dedicated servant of mine for all these years?"

Of course, I thanked Doug for his affirming phone call but replied pretty much the same way Sam did to me. "Doug, I'd love to take some of the credit for what God has done in your life, but you and I both know it was your mom and dad who laid for you the tracks that you've followed and continue to follow to this day. I was a very blessed youth worker who got to ride that train for a short time so that I could encourage you as a mentor and friend. I'm just thankful I didn't blow it!"

PARENTS ARE THE KEY

I love it when I hear from students like Doug. But I can also tell you about students who graduated out of my ministry and probably right out of the church as well. I have no idea if they remained in the faith. My track record is no better than anyone's in that regard. I've never been able to explain why some of my former youth group kids kept on serving Christ as adults and others did not. All I know is that the more I reflect on my career in youth ministry, the more I've come to appreciate the vital role parents play in the spiritual formation of their children. I now realize that much of my ministry has been more like the ministry Paul had with his student Timothy: "I have been reminded of your sincere faith, which first lived in your grandmother Lois and in your mother Eunice and, I am persuaded, now lives in you also" (2 Timothy 1:5). Paul knew exactly who had ignited young Timothy's faith and he acknowledged his subsidiary role as a mere fanner of Timothy's flame.

As a youth worker you will contribute significantly to the spiritual, moral, and social lives of the teens you work with, but parents contribute much more. As my friend Mark DeVries has written: "We can no longer continue to view parents as neutral factors in our ministry to their teenagers. Parents, simply by the way they raise their children, will either empower our ministries or sabotage them. Parents play a role second only to that of the Holy Spirit in building the spiritual foundation of their children's lives."[1]

WE'VE COME A LONG WAY

I've witnessed incredible growth in youth ministry over the years and in some ways have contributed to it. Forty years ago there were hardly any resources for youth workers, so a few of us began writing and publishing books full of youth ministry ideas. There are now dozens of organizations and ministries powering a youth ministry industry that has literally exploded. Go to a youth ministry convention (there are many!) and in the exhibit hall you'll stumble across enough ideas to keep you going for the next ten years. No longer do youth workers have to start their ministries making the same mistakes we made. Now you can get training at hundreds of seminars and conferences that happen every year or go to a Christian college or seminary and get a graduate or postgraduate degree in youth ministry. Youth groups today don't have to pick up their teenagers in old school buses or meet in church basements. Now many of them meet in multimillion-dollar youth complexes outfitted with state-of-the-art sound, lighting, and media technology. We've got bigger and better youth ministry programs, budgets, and staffs than ever before.

TRUTH FROM THE TRENCHES

Parents play a role second only to that of the Holy Spirit in building the spiritual foundation of their children's lives.

But are we getting better results? Are we making disciples of our teenagers? Are we connecting young people to Christ and his church? Are we moving our teens in the direction of becoming "perfect in Christ" (Colossians 1:28) while teaching them to become lifelong followers of Jesus?

We proclaim him . . . so that we may present everyone perfect in Christ. To this end I labor, struggling with all his energy, which so powerfully works in me.

COLOSSIANS 1:28, 29

These are questions that researchers have been asking recently and some of the answers they've found have not been all that encouraging. The Barna Group's researchers, for example, recently surveyed a cross section of twentysomethings and found that of those who had attended church as teenagers, only 39 percent were still "spiritually engaged." And only one out of five said they had maintained a level of spiritual activity consistent with what they did in high school.[2] Another study conducted by LifeWay Research found that the ratio of previously churched students who dropped out of church for at least one year between the ages of 18 and 22 was near 70 percent.[3] In other words, we may be doing bigger and better youth ministry, but we're losing more kids than ever before. It's often said that the youth of today are the church of tomorrow. But there's serious question whether this will indeed be the case. Virtually every denomination—the Church of Jesus Christ of Latter-day Saints (the Mormon Church) is one exception—reports this same trend.[4]

The infamous church dropout rate reportedly ranges anywhere between 80 percent on the high end to 40 percent on the low end—depending on who's conducting the study and who's interpreting the results.[5] While the numbers are frequently debated, there's no denying they're higher than they ought to be, and all this data may be pointing to a systemic weakness in youth ministry as we know it today.

OUR BIGGEST CHALLENGE

Let me say at this point that I don't think there is a direct cause-and-effect relationship between youth ministry and the declining number of young adults who remain connected to the church after their teen years. Youth ministry is not the reason why young people lose their faith or leave the church. There are many forces working against us these days. While youth ministry may serve as a convenient scapegoat, it's not the culprit here. God didn't make a mistake by calling more than a quarter-million adults into youth ministry.[6] Truth be told, we could use a lot more.

But youth ministry is only one part of a twentieth-century trend in the church that has segregated churchgoers according to age and professionalized ministry. This has happened so much that many parents have adopted a kind of drop-off mentality in which they expect the church to do all the spiritual training of their children.

Addressing the problem of teenagers who drop out of church, researcher Christian Smith writes, "The problem is not that the youth won't come to church (most will), or that they hate church (few do), or that they don't want to listen to religious ministers or mature mentoring adults (they will and do)."

The problem instead, Smith says, is that "For decades in many religious traditions, the prevailing model of youth ministry has relied on pulling teens away from their parents."[7]

Smith identifies what I believe are some of the biggest challenges we face in youth ministry today. One is finding ways to integrate teenagers into their faith communities—and that's, in many to most cases, the church—rather than separating the students from those places of faith. But equally, or maybe more important, is figuring out how to bring parents and teens together again to restore the home as the primary place where faith is passed on from one generation to the next. I realize these are no easy tasks. Many of today's parents have grown rather comfortable with the new status quo and just want a place where they can outsource the spiritual training of their kids to someone with the resources, training, and desire to do the job for them.

TRUTH FROM THE TRENCHES

These may be the biggest challenges we face in youth ministry: integrating our students into faith communities—not separating them from such supports—and bringing parents and teens together again to restore the home as the primary place where faith is grown.

TOWARD EFFECTIVE YOUTH MINISTRY

The classic definition of insanity has been doing the same thing over and over and expecting different results each time. If we want different results in youth ministry, then we really can't afford to keep approaching it the same way we've been doing it for the past fifty or so years. I believe one of the most significant ways we can change how we're doing youth ministry is to start doing a better job of engaging parents.

That's what this book is all about. In the chapters that follow I'll give you dozens of ideas and strategies to help you engage parents and work side by side with them to make disciples of their children. But this is not just an idea book. I want you to begin thinking about your youth ministry in a completely new way. Parent ministry is not just another program to add to your already long list of things to do. It has to permeate the very core of your youth ministry philosophy and run as a thread through every youth ministry activity that you do. It all starts with you. As you begin to adjust how you think about parents and how you relate to them, you'll find that your youth ministry culture will also begin to change and parents will become more and more a part of what you do.

I visited recently with Dan, the youth pastor at a church not far from where I live. More than four years ago, Dan made the decision to engage parents as allies and partners in his ministry. "It was like pushing a boulder up a hill," he says of the first two years. "But with time, more and more parents warmed up to the idea and came on board."

Today he says his youth ministry is "powered by parents" and, along with all the parents who are now serving as volunteers and leaders, dozens more are meeting weekly just to pray for the ministry and their kids and to connect with each other. "The change has been remarkable," Dan says of the parents. "And they are really beginning to make a difference in their own homes."

ACTION PLAN

★ How can your ministry better address the two huge youth ministry challenges presented in this chapter? What small changes can you make now to start changing the culture?

THINKING ABOUT PARENTS

When I'm with youth workers I sometimes like to play a little word association game.

"What word or phrase first comes to mind when you think about parents of teenagers?" It's not uncommon to hear, in response, words like . . .

"incompetent"   "disconnected"

"clueless"   "out of touch"

"bad examples"   "critical"

"controlling"   "abusive"

Sounds like parents need a little help with their public image, doesn't it? It's no wonder youth workers don't get all that excited about partnering with parents. Who wants to work with someone who's incompetent, out of touch, or clueless?

Where do those negative images of parents come from?

I'm sure we've all known a few parents (maybe even our own, at times) who fit those descriptions perfectly. But in all fairness, most of them are stereotypes that are probably the result of buying into too much popular culture, including watching too many episodes of *The Simpsons*. Culture, and sometimes even teens themselves, like to perpetuate the my-parent-is-an-idiot mythology—even though nearly every study shows they secretly desire a closer relationship with their parents. One study asked teenagers, "What thing would you most like to change about your family, if anything?" The most common response was "I wish I was closer to my parents." When asked, "Why aren't you closer?", most replied, "I don't know how to do it."[8]

At an Understanding Your Teenager seminar I led recently, the host church youth pastor gave me his take on the large number of parents in attendance. "I don't think I've met most of those parents," he admitted.

"Why not?" I asked.

His reply was strikingly simple. "Well, meeting parents just gets me out of my comfort zone."

I've discovered he's not alone. There are many youth workers who find it difficult to get close to parents. Maybe, like the teens they work with, they just don't know how. Maybe they have an irrational fear of parents. Or maybe they just don't have the time. We'll address some of those issues in this book.

A good place to start, however, is to fully appreciate the vital role that parents play in the lives of their kids. Parents are not perfect by any stretch of the imagination, but they have been uniquely called and gifted to participate fully in the spiritual training of their children. Parents are highly regarded by God—we'll look at a number of Scriptures on this later in this chapter—and they should also be highly regarded by us. By virtue of the fact that they are parents, they bring to the table qualities that we simply can't compete with as youth workers.

TRUTH FROM THE TRENCHES

Among the reasons youth workers have a hard time getting to know the parents of students in their ministries:

- They've never learned this skill; it is not necessarily natural
- They have a fear of parents—rational or irrational
- They believe they don't really have the time

WHAT PARENTS BRING TO THE TABLE
They love their kids more than you do

It's safe to say that you can't love your students the way their parents can. I'll be perfectly honest here. I have never loved a member of my youth group—ever!—like I have loved (and still love) my own kids. There really is no substitute for the incredible depth of parental love.

Of course, someone could argue, we don't have to go far to find parents who don't seem to love their kids—who over-discipline them, verbally or physically abuse them, or fail to give them the time and nurture they need. Bad examples of parental love abound. But the vast majority of parents do love their children—deeply, and far more than we as youth workers do—even when they don't know how to express it very well.

That's why Jesus compared God's love with the love of a parent. In the same way, Paul compared his ministry with the loving relationship a child has with his mother and father (1 Thessalonians 2:6-12). Parents can be a powerful illustration of God's love and care for us. The more we help parents to love their kids well, the better your kids will understand God's love for them. The two are indelibly linked.

As apostles of Christ we could have been a burden to you, but we were gentle among you, like a mother caring for her little children. We loved you so much that we were delighted to share with you not only the gospel of God but our lives as well, because you had become so dear to us. Surely you remember, brothers, our toil and hardship; we worked night and day in order not to be a burden to anyone while we preached the gospel of God to you. You are witnesses, and so is God, of how holy, righteous and blameless we were among you who believed. For you know that we dealt with each of you as a father deals with his own children, encouraging, comforting and urging you to live lives worthy of God, who calls you into his kingdom and glory.

1 THESSALONIANS 2:6-12

They care about their kids more than you do

As youth workers we pride ourselves as people who care about our teens. But I've learned that I can't care about the kids in my youth group like a parent can. I'm ashamed to say that through the years I've let more than a few kids slip through the cracks of my youth ministry. I just didn't do a very good job of including them or making them feel welcome. I may have forgotten their names—and more than once—or, truthfully, never bothered to learn them in the first place.

Parents don't let their kids slip through the cracks. Parents have a vested interest in their children like no one else has. They want their kids to succeed, to get good grades, to be the most popular kid in the school, to get the most attention in the youth group. Some of those desires may not be the greatest things, but parents still want them—they want the best for their own kids. If you've ever coached a little league team, you know how hard it is to deal with parents who think their kids should be in the starting lineup.

While this tendency to care too much can be problematic, it's actually a strength of parenting, not a weakness. Let's go back to that word association game. Here's another response: one of the common complaints I hear from youth workers about involving parents in the ministry is that "parents can't be objective." My answer to this is "Well, that's why you're there." (I'll get into this more in chapter 3.) We can teach parents how to put their nonobjectivity to better use—and they can help us make sure we don't blow it with their kids.

They spend more time with their kids than you do

How much time do you spend with the students in your youth group? Some of us are better at this than others, but even the most dedicated youth workers I know only spend a few hours each week with their students in meetings or after school or at other youth group activities. Parents, on the other hand, spend time with their kids every day, or at least would if they could.

Even with today's busy and disrupted families, parents are generally with their kids much more than we are. We can't possibly compete with parents for time spent with teenagers—nor should we.

They know their kids better than you do

Have you ever had a student walk into your youth group who you knew nothing about? Chances are you make certain assumptions about that student (probably mostly wrong ones) and then, by making small talk and watching him interact with other members of the group, you try to learn more about his personality, friends, needs, and spiritual life. A lot of youth ministry involves this kind of information gathering as we "get to know students."

Truth is, you really don't have to look much farther than a student's parents to get most of the information you need. They know more about their kids than you'll ever find out by trial and error. Parents can be tremendous assets to you. If you want to get to know the kids in your youth group, get to know their parents. The more you know their parents, the more you'll know their kids.

A veteran youth worker and friend of mine tells a story about one of his youth group students—we'll call him Jeremy—who had an unusual personality. Whenever you tried to talk with him, he would start giggling uncontrollably. As you might guess, this made it difficult for Jeremy to make friends and have a serious conversation with anybody. So my friend Jim decided to visit Jeremy's parents to see if he could gain some insight into the boy's strange behavior. When Jim arrived at Jeremy's front door and introduced himself to the father, the man started giggling uncontrollably.

Needless to say, Jim learned a little about Jeremy that day! Parents can become a great wealth of knowledge for you and quite often they're in a much better position to meet the needs of their own kids. As one parent wrote in a parent newsletter, "We live with [our kids] most of the time. You see them for a few hours a week. We appreciate your role with our kids, and there are things that they will share with you that they won't tell us. That's great! They need to have other Christian adults and positive role models involved in their lives. But, please don't make a mistake in thinking that you know our kids better. Partner with us. Don't try to replace us."[9]

TRUTH FROM THE TRENCHES

You don't have to look any further than a student's parents to learn most of what you need to know about that student! Parents can be tremendous assets to your ministry. The more you know the parents, the more you'll know the kids.

They influence their kids more than you do

This is probably the queen mother of all the reasons we have for helping and engaging parents in youth ministry. It's also perhaps the most surprising. For better or for worse, parents not only influence their kids more than you do, they influence their kids more than just about anything—including friends, celebrities, video games, and the rest of pop culture.[10] One recent study asked teenagers who they looked up to the most. Fathers turned out to be three times more popular than celebrities. Mothers were six times more popular![11]

Christian Smith, director of the Center for the Study of Religion and Society at the University of Notre Dame, sums it up pretty well: "Contrary to popular misguided cultural stereotypes and frequent parental misperceptions . . . the evidence clearly shows that the single most important social influence on the religious and spiritual lives of adolescents is their parents. . . . The best social predictor, although not a guarantee, of what the religious and spiritual lives of youth will look like is what the religious and spiritual lives of their parents . . . look like."[12]

My longtime friend and mentor Jay Kesler writes this to parents: "[Your children] learn something new from [you] every day and will live their lives according to the models we give them to follow. So the question we must ask ourselves is 'How can I perform in a competent, mature manner so that when my kids copy me, I will be happy with what I observe in them.'"[13]

Parents, not youth workers, lay down the tracks of faith and values that their children will follow for the rest of their lives. Youth workers and other adult mentors play a lesser but still valuable role in the lives of students as we come alongside parents and families and give them support and encouragement.

They have more authority than you do

Parents more often than not have the final say in what their kids do or don't do. This is especially true for younger teens. Can they go to summer camp? Can they join the worship band? Can they lead a small group? Can they go on a mission trip? In most cases, parents are the people who ultimately make those decisions because they're usually the same people who write the checks.

I've heard many youth workers complain when parents don't allow their kids to participate in certain activities or withhold youth group attendance as a means of disciplining their teenager. I agree that there are times when parents don't make the best decisions regarding discipline. But parents are the only ones who can make those decisions and we need to respect them. Only parents can provide the discipline and boundaries that teenagers need.

They have more responsibility than you do

Who has the responsibility for the evangelism and discipleship of children? Contrary to what many people think, responsibility for those areas was never given to the church or to youth ministry professionals. The responsibility for raising kids in the faith has always rested squarely on the shoulders of parents. From Genesis forward, the Bible teaches us that faith and values get passed from one generation to the next—from parents to children—one family at a time.

- ★ "For I have chosen [Abraham], so that he will direct his children and his household after him to keep the way of the Lord by doing what is right and just" (Genesis 18:19).
- ★ "Only be careful, and watch yourselves closely so that you do not forget the things your eyes have seen or let them slip from your heart as long as you live. Teach them to your children and to their children after them. . . . 'Assemble the people before me to hear my words so that they may learn to revere me as long as they live in the land and may teach them to their children'" (Deuteronomy 4:9, 10).
- ★ "These commandments that I give you today are to be upon your hearts. Impress them on your children. Talk about them when you sit at home and when you walk along the road, when you lie down and when you get up. Tie them as symbols on your hands and bind them on your foreheads. Write them on the doorframes of your houses and on your gates" (Deuteronomy 6:6-9).
- ★ "He decreed statutes for Jacob and established the law in Israel, which he commanded our forefathers to teach their children, so the next generation would know them, even the children yet to be born, and they in turn would tell their children" (Psalms 78:5, 6).
- ★ "Fathers, do not exasperate your children; instead, bring them up in the training and instruction of the Lord" (Ephesians 6:4).

These and many other passages through the Old and New Testaments make it clear that God's plan for the instruction of children in the faith begins in the home. In Luke 2:51, 52 we get a short glimpse into Jesus' adolescence and we see the important role his parents played in his development as a young man, including his choice to be obedient to them.

Then he went down to Nazareth with them [his parents] and was obedient to them. But his mother treasured all these things in her heart. And Jesus grew in wisdom and stature, and in favor with God and men.

LUKE 2:51, 52

As an adolescent, Jesus put himself under the authority and instruction of Mary and Joseph, his earthly parents. It's apparent that Scripture allows us to make the connection that this is what God wants for all children and their parents.

George Barna says it well: "The responsibility for raising spiritual champions, according to the Bible, belongs to parents. The spiritual nurture of children is supposed to take place in the home. Organizations and people from outside the home might support those efforts, but the responsibility is squarely laid at the feet of the family. This is not a job for specialists. It is a job for parents."[14]

LET PARENTS BE PARENTS

Our goal is not to turn parents into youth workers, although some parents may want to get involved as youth leaders and serve on your team of volunteers. Parents bring unique qualities that can be leveraged to raise up the next generation of Christ-followers. Our goal is to encourage, equip, and empower parents to do exactly that.

When we think about parents, the first step is simply to acknowledge that all teens have them. I've found that it's tempting to treat teenagers as if they have no parents at all. This is particularly true with high school students. But unless you have members of your youth group who are living on their own (which you may, but likely very few if so), you can take the number of kids in your group, multiply by two, and that's nearly how many parents—or those acting in the parental role—who are likely connected to your youth ministry in some way. As Mark DeVries notes, "We are foolish to make changes which affect the youth we work with without consulting the people who have the most investment in those [teens]. . . . They are our senior partners here, and they will be doing youth ministry with 'our kids' long after we have gone."[15]

Every home can become an extension of the youth ministry and the youth ministry can be an extension of the home. We can work together with parents to make disciples of their (and our) teens. Wouldn't it be great if everything you were teaching in your youth ministry was being reinforced and put into practice at home? It can happen if we support parents as

THE PROBLEM WITH PIED PIPERS

"Pied Pipers are usually gifted in working with children or teens but simply don't have the interest or desire to bridge their ministry to the home. Through their dynamic and charismatic leadership, they're able to draw a crowd of students to follow them. Yet in many cases, Pied Pipers see parents as a disruption to the work they're trying to do. Unfortunately, they don't realize that their success or influence is only temporary, and sometimes these leaders need to be removed from their positions in order for the faith at home vision to succeed."

— *Mark Holmen*, Building Faith at Home *(Ventura, CA: Regal Books, 2007), p. 140* much as we expect them to support us and if we teach teens to honor and respect their parents as the Bible calls them to.

ACTION PLAN

★ Why is it easy to create stereotypes of parents? Why is this a dangerous game to play?

★ Do you struggle with getting to know the parents of your students? If so, why?

THINKING ABOUT YOUTH WORKERS

When I first started doing youth ministry about four decades ago, my role was pretty much that of a teen magnet. I was only a few years older than most of the students in my youth group and, in the vernacular of the day, I was "groovy." I could play the guitar, sing folk songs, tell jokes, lead games, perform skits, and keep the kids hanging around long enough to slip in a relevant gospel message and teach what little I knew about the Bible and living the Christian life.

One of my mentors in youth ministry, Jay Kesler, used to call youth workers like me "bright young men." Just as light bulbs attract bugs, so bright young men attract teenagers. Every church in those days needed a bright young man to keep kids buzzing around the church. It worked great except for the fact that light bulbs frequently burn out. Whenever that would happen, the bugs would fly away and the church would have to go find another light bulb, another bright young man (or woman) with enough charisma and youth appeal to bring the kids back. That's essentially the cycle that has been repeated by thousands of churches and youth organizations through the years to keep their youth groups stocked with kids.

While remnants of the bright young man model of youth ministry still exist, most of today's youth ministries have moved to a more relational emphasis. The role of the youth worker is no longer that of entertainer or activity director but rather that of the mentor, adult friend, and spiritual guide. This has been a positive shift that's enabled more people to get involved in youth ministry than ever before, including more volunteer adults.

THE CHANGING ROLE OF THE YOUTH WORKER

But the role of the youth worker continues to evolve. The more we learn about the spiritual formation of teenagers and the crucial role that parents and families play in their spiritual and moral development, the more important it is for youth workers to engage parents. Youth workers of the future must no longer work only with teenagers but must work with and engage their parents and families as well.

This is particularly true for youth workers who are in a position of leadership in the church, whether professional (paid staff) or volunteer. From the biblical point of view, the role of a leader in the church is that of a team builder, a coach, and one who motivates and trains other people for ministry "so that the body of Christ may be built up" (Ephesians 4:12). In youth ministry terms, those being built up include parents and other adults in the church as well as the teenagers. This sometimes comes as unwelcome news to youth workers who don't feel qualified to work with parents and who see this as an added burden to their already busy ministry workload.

It was [Christ] who gave some to be . . . pastors and teachers, to prepare God's people for works of service, so that the body of Christ may be built up.

EPHESIANS 4:11, 12

But engaging parents in youth ministry doesn't have to become another burden on your back, another plate to spin. Instead it can become a way to insure longevity and stability in your ministry and to insure better long-term outcomes. You can and should continue to work with teenagers, of course. But you can only lead by example. Working with parents doesn't mean you have to become a family pastor or a certified counselor. And it doesn't mean you have to become dull and boring. But the days of the superstar youth worker—the bright young man or woman—are over. The youth ministry of the future must be a partnership with parents.

WHAT YOUTH WORKERS BRING TO THE TABLE

So after reading chapter two, you may be wondering if there is any importance left in your role! Maybe we should just fire all the youth workers in the church and put all the parents in charge.

That would be a bad idea. Parents need all the help they can get and besides, parents and youth workers play complementary roles. I have always encouraged parents to support the youth ministry of their church because teenagers naturally seek out adults, mentors, and role models outside the home who will understand them, take them seriously, and treat them with dignity and respect. If they can't find people like that in the church, they will probably look elsewhere. That's why teenagers are so vulnerable to celebrity worship. They are looking for heroes who are not their parents.

Here are a few ways youth workers can be heroes not only to kids but also to their parents.

You can be more objective than parents can

Youth workers can be a lot more objective than parents. This is the flip side of parents caring so much about their kids. They just don't have enough distance between themselves and their kids to be objective.

TRUTH FROM THE TRENCHES

Teenagers will look to *someone* for a role model, a hero, someone to respect. It's one reason they're so vulnerable to celebrity worship. Teens are looking for heroes who are not their parents.

I remember a former student of mine—I'll call him Billy—who was always skipping school and flunking many of his courses. He wanted to become a truck driver some day (which he eventually did) and considered high school to be a complete waste of his time. Billy was afraid to talk to his parents about the situation—they always went ballistic over such talk—but he was comfortable talking with me. I was able to help him—and his parents—because I was able to be objective. And truthfully, if I were Billy's father, I'm sure I'd have gone ballistic over some of his actions as well!

You don't have to hang around teenagers too long these days to hear some pretty outrageous things in a group discussion or just in regular conversation. Fortunately, I've learned the fine art of keeping my composure when kids say something really stupid or launch an f-bomb in the room. Not too many parents can do that. Assuming that their kid would talk at all when the parents are around, most parents find it extremely difficult to resist correcting or scolding their child for saying things that are off-base or inappropriate.

As a parent I've always been thankful that my kids had other adults in their lives who were more objective than I could be and who were there to be sounding boards for their thoughts and ideas. Teenagers need adults with that kind of objectivity and grace.

You understand the world of teenagers better than they do

Many if not most youth workers pay attention to youth culture and quite often live in it themselves. If you work with kids, you probably try to stay on top of the latest trends in music, technology, clothing, movies, social networking and other online sites, TV shows, games, celebrities, research, and the like. You may even have the hair, clothes, and tattoos to prove it.

Parents, on the other hand, tend to be afraid of youth culture and have a hard time understanding why their teens want to act, look, and behave the way they do. That makes it difficult not only for parents to help their kids make wise choices, but a challenge to communicate with them at all. As a youth worker, you can form an important bridge between the world of teen culture and the world of parents.

You can be a better friend than parents can

I frequently tell parents that the three most important things to a teenager are: 1) friends, 2) friends, and 3) friends. As most people know, friends are the life-blood of adolescence. Teenagers have a developmental need to separate from their parents and establish identities of their own. Friends provide affirmation and acceptance, both of which are crucial to the process of identity formation and integration with the world outside the home.

I encourage parents to spend time with their kids and keep a strong relationship with them, but I also tell them that it's not their job to be their best friend. Almost without exception, teens prefer parents to be parents—providing love, security, and guidance, saying no, setting limits, and making the tough decisions that they (or their friends) can't always make.

Youth workers, on the other hand, can't be parents but they can be friends. Teenagers want and need adult friends every bit as much as they want and need peer friends. Just as friends are the lifeblood of adolescence, friends are also the lifeblood of youth ministry—but this time in the form of adults who are willing to come alongside teens and be their friends. That's something youth workers can do that parents can't.

You can communicate with teenagers better than they can

While children listen attentively to their parents, teenagers generally *listen less and watch more*. Parents influence their teenagers best by modeling. When parents talk to their teenagers, even the calmest, wisest dad or mom can sound like a fingernail on a blackboard.

Youth workers, however, are often skilled youth communicators. Even if you aren't comfortable giving youth talks or teaching a class, your willingness to speak truth into the lives of kids is a real gift to parents. Youth workers in the church can provide a neutral, nonjudgmental voice that teens will listen to and trust. Today's kids need youth workers who will communicate the gospel to them in a way they can understand. Teens listen attentively to voices outside the home and if they don't have a voice like yours, they'll listen to any voice they can find. We can play a vital role in supporting what parents teach their kids at home. Often they'll listen to us when they won't listen to their parents.

TRUTH FROM THE TRENCHES

Even if you aren't comfortable giving youth talks or teaching a class, your willingness to speak truth into the lives of kids is a gift to parents. You play a vital role in supporting what parents teach their kids at home as well.

You can provide a caring community for teenagers better than parents can

Youth workers can help teenagers get plugged into a positive peer environment that will provide them with acceptance and affirmation. Parents worry constantly about their teenagers' choice of friends. They remember how powerful friendships can be and they know that when they were teenagers they made some poor friendship choices—with the result often being serious trouble.

Parents choose playmates for their young children, but they can't choose friends for their teens. Friends are very personal to a teenager, who quite often chooses friends by trial and error. Youth workers can help teenagers with this process and help them get connected with a supportive faith community of mentors and peers who share their values and faith and want to be their friends. That's what the youth group is there for.

BUILDING MUTUAL TRUST AND RESPECT

A partnership with parents has to be built on a solid foundation of mutual trust and respect that can only be developed with time. Remember that we are asking a lot of parents—to trust us with their most prized possessions. Middle school pastor Kurt Johnston points out that success or failure in youth ministry depends entirely on two things: the sovereignty of God and the support of parents.[16] If parents can't trust us with their kids, we're in big trouble.

Here are a few ways to build trust with parents:

★ Communicate regularly (more on this in chapter 7). It's a mistake to call on parents only when you need something or have bad news to report.

★ Don't treat them as problems to be solved or obstacles to overcome. Think of parents as partners and assets.

★ Act like an adult. I know, it's hard to walk the line between relating to teenagers and relating to adults, but don't let incarnational youth ministry[17] distance you from parents. Parents sometimes have a hard time trusting an adult who acts and looks like a teenager. Wear clothes that aren't too extreme, go easy on the tattoos and piercings, choose a hairdo that even grown-ups like, and learn to talk in complete sentences.

★ Be professional. Not in the sense of "I'm a professional; don't try this at home." Rather: "I'm a professional and you can trust me to show up on time and make sure we have safe tires on the van and reservations at the campground."

★ Don't do really dumb things like showing R-rated movie clips at your youth meetings or having your kids play games that involve chain saws.

★ Stick around for a while. Trust comes with time. Successful, sustainable youth ministries often take years to establish and have leaders with longevity and continuity.

You have more resources than they do

Most parents will admit they're clueless about adolescent development, youth culture, youth ministry, and parenting. They need help and don't know where to find it. But youth workers have access to all kinds of resources and training that can help parents and kids understand each other better. Later in this book

I'll give you ideas for equipping parents with valuable resources and ideas that they can't find anywhere else.

You can involve teenagers in ministry easier than parents can

Parents have a hard enough time getting their kids to clean their rooms, let alone getting them to serve others and become involved in ministry. But youth workers can motivate teenagers to discover their unique talents and gifts by getting them involved in mission projects, youth group leadership, and other ministry opportunities. Teenagers learn best by doing and a youth group can provide teens with a place where they can put their faith into action.

ACTION PLAN

★ You can connect and communicate with your teens, in many cases, better than their parents can. Think through how you can use that ability to both honor parents and build up kids— at the same time.

THINKING THROUGH INVOLVING PARENTS

★ Were you involved in a youth group as a teenager? If so, what was it like?

★ Who or what had the biggest influence on your faith and values as a teenager?

★ What kind of "results" should a youth ministry expect to have? Will those desired results be better if you involve parents?

★ The Old Testament gave the responsibility for raising godly children to parents. But one could argue: "The Old Testament was written thousands of years ago. The writers couldn't possibly have understood the challenges that parents face today." Do you agree or disagree with this sentiment?

★ What do you think are the primary responsibilities of a church youth leader or youth pastor?

PART TWO

PUTTING IT TOGETHER

PUTTING TOGETHER A PARTNERSHIP

Youth workers and parents each bring different assets to the table of youth ministry and they each play different roles in the lives of teenagers.

But they share a common goal.

Every parent's desire is for their children to grow up to become the young men and women God created them to be. When my kids were young, I remember reading the description of the young Jesus in Luke 2:52: "And [he] grew in wisdom and stature, and in favor with God and men." That's exactly what I wanted for my children—that they would grow strong intellectually, physically, spiritually, and socially. I used to insert the names of my children in that verse and read it out loud. I know that all parents have similar hopes and dreams for their children.

At parenting seminars I sometimes ask parents to write down some of the goals they have for their kids. I'll ask: "What do you want for your children? Beyond things like making the football team or cheerleading squad, getting good grades, getting a college degree, getting a high-paying job . . . what are the really important qualities of life and qualities of character that you want your children to someday have?"

Almost always the parents write down things like . . .

★ We want (our son or daughter) to love and follow Jesus.
★ We want (our son or daughter) to have healthy relationships with other people.

★   We want (our son or daughter) to learn to make good choices based on scriptural principles.

★   We want (our son or daughter) to use his/her gifts and talents to serve Christ, the church, and the world.

★   We want (our son or daughter) to glorify God and enjoy him forever.

After parents make this list, I ask an even tougher question: "Now, what are you currently doing, or what do you plan to do in the future, to help your teenager reach those goals?" This is where parents often get stumped. They aren't sure exactly what they can do. For many—too many—the solution is to drop their kids off at the youth group. They simply outsource the job to you, the youth worker.

And we've been more than happy to take on that responsibility. We say to parents: "Yes, your goals are our goals! Send your kids to us and we'll make disciples out of them."

But what we've learned over the years is that we can't accomplish those goals without the help of parents. Neither can parents do it by themselves. That's why God created the church.

PARTNERING WITH PARENTS

Whenever I tell parents that the Bible gives the primary responsibility for the spiritual growth of their children to them, not the church, I'm always struck not only by the awesome weight of the task I've just discussed with them, but also by how impossible it sounds. And I can just hear their thoughts: *When in the world am I supposed to fit that into my family's schedule? . . . How can I expect my kids to talk to me about God when they won't even talk to me about the weather? . . . I don't know anything about the Bible. . . . Isn't that what we pay our youth pastor to do?*

I can't blame parents for not feeling up to this. When my kids were teenagers I didn't feel very qualified either. I have been both the parent of a teenager *and* a youth worker and I can tell you that, as a parent, I desperately needed youth workers to come alongside my kids. And, as a youth worker, I desperately needed parents to do what only parents can do. Youth workers can't become surrogate parents. That's why youth workers and parents must form a partnership—a real relationship that allows both parents and youth workers to do what they do best.

Partnering with parents in youth ministry is not a new concept. This isn't the first book to suggest it—far from it. In fact, it's almost become the hot new trend in youth ministry. But few youth workers are having much success with any form of partnership because parent ministry is frequently regarded as just another program to add to an already packed youth ministry schedule.

When I talk to youth workers about partnering with parents, I can just hear some of *their* thoughts: *How am I supposed work with parents when my job is to work with kids? . . . When am I going to find the time to hold parent meetings and publish a parent newsletter or put on a parent seminar? . . . How can I expect parents to pay any attention to me when I've never had teenagers of my own?*

Those are all valid questions and I'll try to address some of them in this chapter. But let me say first that they stem from a misunderstanding of what it means to engage parents in youth ministry. Partnering with parents really isn't about adding more things to your to-do list. It simply means acknowledging with humility that we can't win with kids unless parents are winning too. If we truly believe that, it will impact everything we're doing, from top to bottom.

In his book *Building Faith at Home*, Mark Holmen describes the "add-a-silo" model of ministry in the church, which is probably the most common way we get things done today. Whenever the church identifies a need, it creates a new program (a silo) to meet it.[18] That's why we have so many ministries in the church, including youth ministry, which often run entirely independent from each other. We do it that way because that's what we're used to doing.

By contrast, Holmen suggests a better way to serve parents and families and I think it applies here. Rather than building another silo—and adding another program to be maintained—what if you were to change all your existing programs a little bit? What if every one of them engaged parents and helped parents in some way to leverage their immense influence and the love they have for their kids? This would be a whole new way of thinking about a partnership with parents that would impact everything you do. For example . . .

★ If you're planning a youth group mission trip, open it up to parents.
★ If you're doing a discussion on sex and relationships, give parents the opportunity to share with their kids what they believe on the subject.
★ If you're having a night of fun and games, invite parents either as players or referees.

The last thing you need to do is to create another program that's separate from all the others. On the other hand, you may find that some of your existing programs need to be eliminated or changed significantly because they undermine your partnership with parents. For example . . .

★ If your youth ministry conducts a youth worship service that prevents your teens from worshiping with their parents and the rest of the church, you may want to move that time to another time or do away with it altogether. There's great value in your teens worshiping *with* their parents, observing and sharing different styles of worship.
★ If some of your programs or events are so expensive that they create a hardship for families, cancel those events or find a way to get them subsidized by the church.
★ If you have so many programs that they put stress on family schedules, reducing the time parents can spend with their teens, it's best to cut back.
★ If you are so busy running programs that you have no time to meet and engage the parents of your teens, that's a good clue that you probably have too many programs (or need a good book on time management!).

A true partnership with parents isn't about adding new programs so much as it is thinking differently about the programs that already exist.

TRUTH FROM THE TRENCHES

You may find that some of your existing programs need to be eliminated or changed significantly because they undermine your partnership with parents. A true partnership isn't adding new programs; it's thinking differently about the programs that already exist.

Obviously, this approach will get a lot more traction in a church where the entire congregation, including the senior pastor and the rest of the church leadership, is committed to equipping the home as the primary place where faith is nurtured. I admit that one of the obstacles many youth ministries face is that the ministry finds itself as a silo—just one of many other stand-alone programs in the church. It stands alongside the children's ministry, singles ministry, men's ministry, women's ministry, maybe even a family ministry—each of which have different objectives and may be competing with each other for attention, resources, volunteers, and time on the church calendar.

If that's the case, remember that movements most often begin with a small group and spread out to a larger group over time. Rarely does change begin with the large group and move down to the small group. If you can implement a family-based, family-friendly partnership with parents in your ministry, it can and will begin to impact the rest of the church. If you're having success with it in the junior high ministry, it can spread to the high school ministry, down to the children's ministry, over to the adult ministries, and so on.

ANY QUESTIONS?

Before we go any further, let me field some of the questions you're surely thinking right about now:

"What if I just don't have time for working with parents?"

Most of us find time to do the things that are important to us. If encouraging and equipping parents to be spiritual leaders at home seems important to you, you'll make the time to do it. Mark DeVries puts it this way: "Youth ministry at its best involves a continual process of setting and adjusting priorities, of deciding what we will wring our hands about and what we will let slide. And let's face it, ministry to or through parents of teenagers has simply been one of the many things on our to-do list that we've had to let slide."[19]

The only way to stop the slide is to give it a higher priority. If you consider a partnership with parents as optional, it's unlikely to ever happen. But when God gives you a passion for helping parents and families and makes it a critical part of your vision—see my thoughts on prayer in the next chapter—he'll also provide the time.

"What if my job description doesn't specify that I work with parents?"

If you were hired (or volunteered) to work with teenagers, then by all means keep on working with them. You don't have to become a family minister or a minister to adults to work with parents. No change in your job description is needed.

Just remember that if your vision, mission, or job description includes making disciples of Christ of your teenagers (hopefully it does), then working with parents is a necessity. If your job description included "taking the youth group on a ski trip to Colorado" and you learned that parents could provide you with the money, ski gear, and condos to pull it off, you'd have no problem working with parents, would you?

"What if I'm the voice crying in the wilderness"?

If you're the only one who seems to care about a ministry to and through parents, start slow. Find a few others who might be interested in learning how to engage parents in youth ministry. Encourage them to read this book or others like Mark DeVries's *Family-Based Youth Ministry* or Mark Holmen's *Building Faith at Home*. Get one other person to share your vision and it will begin to spread and grow.

Maybe your church is so locked into an age-segregated model of youth ministry that it's resistant to change of any kind. Don't be discouraged. You can soften the resistance by introducing a few family-based concepts slowly over time. Chapter 5 will give you a few guidelines for getting a ministry to parents (as well as a ministry with the help of parents) off the ground. Take baby steps and remember that something is always better than nothing.

"What if I suffer from 'parent-phobia' —a fear of working with parents?"

Well, you're not alone. Many youth workers are afraid of parents or just lack the confidence to work with them. When I started doing parent seminars,

I was terrified by the prospect that those in attendance might disagree with me or ask me a question I couldn't answer. It took several years before I realized that parents were just as insecure and unsure of themselves as I was. Actually, they were probably more afraid of me than I was of them! If you'll take the first steps to form an alliance with parents, as awkward as those steps may be, you'll find that parents are very forgiving and grateful for your willingness to serve.

Fear often comes from misunderstanding or a lack of understanding. That's one of the reasons why I created the Understanding Your Teenager seminars to help parents. When parents understand a few of the basics of adolescent development, they'll be less fearful and more proactive as parents. Youth workers study the world of adolescence to learn all they can about the age group they're working with. If you want to get more comfortable around parents, learn all you can about them. Parents belong to a specific demographic group with unique developmental characteristics and needs just like teenagers. You can learn about parents pretty much the same way you learn about kids: spend time with them, ask questions, be humble, and listen to what they have to say. Take some surveys. Read a few books about parents and about parenting—even if you don't have any kids of your own.[20] You'll get a glimpse into their world and the issues they're facing. The more you learn about them and learn to think like them, the more comfortable and better equipped you'll be to work successfully with them.

TRUTH FROM THE TRENCHES

Begin with the small steps in your efforts to start an alliance with parents. As awkward as those steps might be, you'll find that parents are very forgiving and grateful for what you're doing.

"What if parents simply don't want to get involved with the youth ministry?"

Welcome to youth ministry in the twenty-first century. You've probably just described the majority of parents. Most are quite content to drop their kids off and let you teach them everything they need to know about God. Others are just too busy, and some don't care. It will probably take some time for a critical mass of parents to become partners with you in youth ministry.

My advice is to be patient with parents. Don't give up on them. Continue to communicate with all your parents and take what you can get. Don't take rejection personally—this is very important—and don't let those who refuse to get involved set the agenda for everyone else. Just be thankful for those parents who do get involved and give them plenty of encouragement. Remember, if you have one parent involved this year and four parents a year from now, that's a 400 percent gain!

MEMO: TO MY TEEN'S YOUTH WORKER
FROM: A GRATEFUL PARENT

★ First of all, thanks for being there for my kids.

★ I'd like to get to know you. Call me up sometime. Maybe we can do lunch.

★ I'm willing to get involved and help out if you'll give me something to do that doesn't embarrass me—or my kids.

★ Let me know what's going on with the youth group from time to time because my kids never tell me squat.

★ I really would like to be the best parent in the world, so if you know of resources that would be helpful, I'd sure appreciate them.

★ And again, thanks for being there for my kids.

"What if some of the kids in my youth group don't have Christian parents?"

You can still reach out to those parents without making them feel uncomfortable. Some unbelieving parents may be suspicious of church leaders (and rightfully so) because they've heard stories about clergy abuse and religious cults that alienate young people from their parents. Don't be afraid to make contact with these parents and answer any questions they might have. It may take some time to build trust and mutual respect with unbelieving parents, but they shouldn't be excluded from your efforts to partner with parents.

Treat unbelieving parents just like you would any other parent in your ministry. Find ways to encourage them and connect them to other parents. (I'll have more on this in Chapter 9.) Invite them to parent seminars that might be appropriate for them and encourage them to be involved in other activities that don't require a profession of faith. Use the opportunities in front of you to teach your teens to honor their parents even if they don't believe as we do.

"Honor your father and mother"—which is the first commandment with a promise—
"that it may go well with you and that you may enjoy long life on the earth."

EPHESIANS 6:2, 3

Keep in mind that many parents can be reached through the youth ministry of the church. I have a good friend named Jim who was led to Christ by his sixteen-year-old daughter. She became a Christian and was encouraged by her youth group leader to honor her parents, pray for them daily, and live for Christ at home. Jim later gave his life to Christ and is now growing in his faith and determined to be for his daughter the example he failed to be when she was younger. This doesn't happen with all parents, of course, but it *can* happen when we pray for them, treat them with love and respect, and teach our kids to do the same.

A final point on this: when you're doing events that bring adults and teens together, be sensitive to the students who may feel left out because their parents aren't there. There's always a possibility (if not a probability) that you'll have students in your youth ministry who don't live with their parents. They may live in a foster family or with their grandparents. Their parents may have died or for some other reason can't be involved in their lives. Mark Holmen points out that there are about twenty-five different kinds of families represented in most congregations. Be sensitive to the needs of all your teens and, if possible, provide stand-in parents in the form of youth leaders or other parents who are willing to take that role. And again, don't let parents who can't or won't be involved set the agenda for how you do youth ministry.

ACTION PLAN

★ What can change in your ministry to allow you to include parents more? Remember, you're not adding another silo; find already-defined programs that can benefit from more parental involvement.

PUTTING TOGETHER A PLAN

Every year I try planting a small vegetable garden out behind our house. I've learned that if I want to get delicious homegrown tomatoes, corn, carrots, peas, squash, and string beans, there are a few things I absolutely have to do. First, I have to prepare the soil by turning it with a rototiller. I also need to add certain nutrients, like compost and fertilizer. Then, usually in late winter—yes, we do have winter in California—I plant the seeds at just the right depth. After weeks and sometimes months of daily watering and cultivating, I finally get the harvest I want. And for years, when my kids were still at home, they were forced to eat zucchini every night for about two months straight.

Now there have been some years when, in a rush, I tried to skip a few of these steps. I didn't prepare the soil properly. Or, like a dummy, I planted the garden and then failed to take care of it. Sometimes I assumed that somebody else (like one of my kids) would. In any case, my vegetable plants frequently suffered from malnutrition and dehydration, leading me to the discovery that wilted or dead tomato plants don't produce many tomatoes.

This bit of agricultural wisdom is called the law of the farm and, of course, also applies to most of life. Simply put, if you want good results, you have to do the work required to get those results. There really aren't any short cuts in farming—or most anything else that's worthwhile.

NO EASY BUTTONS

I know one youth pastor who caught the family-based youth ministry bug at a recent conference and then went back to his church and changed everything overnight. He nuked the youth group and started preaching parent sermons, publishing parent newsletters, scheduling parent seminars, and organizing parent small groups. He expected everyone in the church to jump on board, but they just jumped all over him instead. He expected a parent revival but got a parent revolt.

I met recently with another youth worker who was on the verge of giving up his parent-inclusive approach to ministry. "Honestly, this is the toughest thing I've ever tried to do in my ministry career," he said. "I try to come alongside parents and all I get is more complaints and criticism. I don't know if it's worth it."

It's worth it—but it's not easy. You can find an easy button at the office supply stores, but you won't find any in youth ministry, or in this book. But before you start trying out the ideas in the next section it's wise to do a little soil preparation first. Remember that great ideas don't always produce great results. Weeds need to be cleared, ground needs to be tilled, and fertilizer needs to be applied. And when you spread fertilizer around, some people will object to the aroma. I've discovered that when you try to solve problems or bring about positive changes in the church, things not only take time, they sometimes get worse before they get better. But they *do* get better when you stay the course and tend to the garden.

IT STARTS WITH YOU

I've had the opportunity to visit hundreds of youth ministries in churches all over the country in recent years. Some have a lot of parent participation in the ministry and others don't. What makes the difference? It's pretty simple, really. Churches with strong parent partnerships have somebody who is totally committed to the concept and leading the way in implementing it. Maybe that *somebody* in your church is you.

Let me encourage you to learn all you can about helping parents. Don't just stop with reading this book. Seek out other voices that also are calling for a family-based approach to youth ministry (there are many!). Talk to other youth workers, visit their churches, ask a lot of questions, and glean all you can from their experiences. Attend conferences and seminars that promote parent and family ministry. I'm confident that the more you learn about helping parents, the more excited you'll become about it. When God gives you the vision, passion, and commitment for parent ministry, you will inspire others and make it happen in your church.

MAKING IT PERSONAL

When I'm talking to youth workers about ministry to and through parents, it sometimes occurs to me that the blank looks I'm seeing on their faces probably stem from the fact that they haven't learned to be spiritual leaders at home themselves. It's not easy to lead someone to a place you haven't been yourself.

If you don't have children—or even if you're single—hang in through this section because it's still important. (And chances are you will have kids at some point in the future!) You don't have to be a perfect parent to encourage and help families, of course. But it's a sad fact that many youth workers and pastors avoid talking to parents about being spiritual leaders at home because it hits a little too close to *their* home.

Some youth workers are hesitant to work with parents because their own family lives are a mess. They feel guilty and defeated as parents themselves. It's not unusual to hear something like this: "I deal with ministry stuff all day at church and just don't have the time and energy to do it at home, too." It's no wonder that sometimes the children of clergy are stereotyped as being unruly and out of control. But Paul reminds us (1 Timothy 3:4, 5; Titus 1:6) that being a faithful parent in teaching our own kids is an important principle for leaders in the church, including a requirement for some.

He [an elder or deacon] must manage his own family well and see that his children obey him with proper respect. (If anyone does not know how to manage his own family, how can he take care of God's church?)

1 TIMOTHY 3:4, 5

Let's be honest. There are many of us who have failed in this regard. I'm fortunate that my wife and children still love me and are doing well in spite of the fact that I was often doing ministry at the expense of my family. It's a common disease in ministry—the disease of busyness. We do good work, but it's not the most important work. Our first responsibility is to take care of our own house. As Joshua put it, "As for me and my household, we will serve the Lord" (Joshua 24:15). We can't lead people down a road that we aren't willing to travel ourselves.

I can tell you from experience that when your youth ministry days are over, the only kids you'll wish you spent more time with are your own. In a bit of over-statement, perhaps, Doug Fields writes, "When your youth ministry days are over, nobody will thank you or even remember what you did for their kids. The only thing you'll be left with is what you've built into your own personal life, into your own family."[21] That's not to say that our youth ministry days aren't going to have an impact. On the contrary, God blesses everything we do (regardless) and our ministries bear fruit in ways we often never anticipate or realize. But our first responsibility is to take care of our own families and to raise our children in the "training and instruction of the Lord" (Ephesians 6:4).

TRUTH FROM THE TRENCHES

One of the most common diseases in ministry is the disease of busyness. We do good work, but it's not the most important work. Our first responsibility is to take care of our own families and to raise our children in the Lord.

ONE STEP AT A TIME

As we move forward with this idea of a partnership with parents, it's important to remember that change takes time and you can only get there one step at a time. It's a little bit like trying to change the course of a cruise ship. If you're the captain, you don't want try any quick and sudden turns. If you do, you'll either capsize the boat or send all the tables in the dining hall sliding across the floor, along with the passengers who will want to throw you overboard as soon as they get back on their feet. To change the course of a cruise ship—or a church—it's best to do it just a few degrees at a time.

Here are a few steps that will help you get your youth ministry headed in the right direction. You don't have to take them in order and you certainly don't have to try to implement them all at once.

Pray like crazy

I list this first but it should be included at every step of the way. Seek God's wisdom and guidance as you implement any of the ideas in this book. Working with parents is not easy or predictable—at all. You'll need supernatural power to achieve success. Pray continually for direction and everyone who will be involved—your teens, the parents, your leaders, yourself. Remember that by definition this approach to youth ministry requires an acknowledgement that you can't do any of this by yourself. Jesus had this attitude (John 5:19); why would we want to be any different?

Find out who the parents are

Before missionaries go to the mission field, they spend a considerable amount of time studying the people group they will be serving. Effective youth workers generally do the same with the student population. We learn everything we can about kids and the culture they live in. So here's an important shift in thinking: your mission field will now include parents as well. Before you start making changes, take time to learn all you can about the parents and families of the teens and preteens in your youth ministry. Who are they? What are their needs? You can learn a lot by listening to parents, getting to know their names, asking questions, talking to kids, visiting homes, taking surveys, and the like.

Bring other leaders on board

If you want to avoid that "voice crying in the wilderness" syndrome we talked about earlier, take time to sell your vision for parent ministry to other church leaders. Make sure the senior pastor, especially, is on board. I think it's safe to say that if the senior pastor doesn't know what's going on or, worse, doesn't agree with what you're doing, your efforts may be finished even before they get started.

Let me say here that most pastors today understand how important it is to get parents more involved in the spiritual nurture of their kids at home. One of the most exciting trends in church ministry today is the Faith at Home movement that's getting a good deal of attention at leadership and pastors conferences across North America and around the world.[22]

Just as you can't plant a garden until the climate properly changes, so you can't proceed with an effective ministry to and with parents until there's a warming to the idea on the part of other church leaders. What you do in the youth ministry will impact other ministries in the church: the men's ministry, the women's ministry, the children's ministry, small group leaders, Sunday school teachers, church boards, the finance committee—the whole congregation. This is the kind of soil preparation that will take time, patience, and maybe even a little diplomacy.

Form a study/prayer group

Before you move forward with writing mission statements and implementing programs, you might consider pulling together a core group of leaders who will spend some time praying together and studying various aspects of parent and family ministry. I would recommend that you read a book together (like this one) or perhaps one by the two Marks—Mark DeVries and Mark Holmen. DeVries's *Family-Based Youth Ministry* has become a youth ministry classic and Holmen's *Building Faith at Home* has led to the movement to get parents back in the game as the primary spiritual trainers of their children. There are other excellent resources as well that you can use for guidance as you continue with your plans.

Rewrite the mission statement

At the very least, you may want to take a second look at the mission statement (if you have one) for your youth ministry to see how it speaks to a partnership with parents. (Don't have such a statement? Now's a great time to start drafting one.) Are parents included in your statement? Does your youth ministry exist to serve parents as well as teenagers? If your mission statement doesn't explicitly say something about these things, you might want to do a little rewriting.

This might be a good time to mention that you don't have to change everything. If you've adopted a "purpose driven" ministry philosophy, for example, there's no reason why you can't include parents in any or all of the main spiritual elements you're focusing on.

The most important thing is to make sure your mission statement doesn't exclude parents altogether or communicate that the youth ministry can do it all without them.

EXAMPLES:

Inadequate mission statement:
Our youth ministry exists to reach teenagers for Christ and to make disciples of them by teaching God's Word, building community, and involving students in mission and service.

Far better mission statement:
Our youth ministry exists to reach teenagers for Christ and to make disciples of them by empowering parents, teaching God's Word, building community, and involving students and families in mission and service.

Evaluate existing programs

It might be a good time to take a hard look at your youth ministry programs to decide what's worth keeping and what needs to be cut. Make a list of everything you're doing in the ministry and then evaluate and prioritize. Remember that plants don't grow merely from being planted; they also have to be pruned. Don't add anything to your already busy schedule without making room for it with some well thought-out cutting. Remember that anytime you cut something out, someone will probably object. I once lost my job at a church for unilaterally cutting a Bible quiz competition that had been in place for years before I got there. I learned that sometimes you need to be careful when making changes, even with seemingly small things.

Set some achievable long- and short-term goals

Create goals for your youth ministry. Here are some suggestions:

Long-term objectives: two years and beyond

★ Teach your teens to understand, honor, and bless their parents. Give them a healthy and positive view of the home, of marriage, and family.

★ Teach parents to understand and stay connected to their teenagers so that kids want their parents' faith.

★ Inspire and motivate parents to have regular faith conversations at home with their children.

★ Give parents tools and teach them skills for passing their faith on to their kids.

★ Give families more opportunities to experience God together in worship, service, and recreation as a family unit rather than individually.

Short-term action steps: to accomplish this year

★ Contact every parent personally in person or by phone. Communicate the most important things, talk to them about their teen, and invite them to come by the ministry or your office anytime for a visit. Follow up with an e-mail.

★ Schedule a parent seminar.

★ Do a Bible study/teaching series with your teens on parent-teen relationships.

★ Start a parents-of-teenagers small group or Sunday school class.

★ Create a parent newsletter (the best suggestion is to start it on a quarterly basis).

★ Invite twelve parents to become volunteer leaders.

★ Plan a family mission trip.

★ Create take-home discussion starters for at least one lesson per month.

Make the effort a priority in your budget

A sure indicator of how serious your ministry is about helping parents succeed at home is the amount of money that's been committed to this priority. Jesus put it this way: "For where your treasure is, there your heart will be also" (Matthew 6:21). Resources, seminars, and other special events for parents and families usually involve some expenses; if the money's not there, they're unlikely to happen. Put pen to paper and start doing the math. If your youth ministry budget for the year is $20,000, allocate $5,000 of that for parenting resources. Don't have it? If you can successfully cast a vision for helping parents win with their kids at home, you can probably find—or raise—the funding to make it happen.

Articulate your vision

Communicate your vision for parents and families to the congregation—to the parents, your students, and the rest of the church. Keep talking about it and find ways to give it visibility in the church. You won't succeed by making one presentation or sending out a mailing or two. If possible, ask the pastor to preach a sermon or, better yet, a series of sermons on the family and parenting, reinforcing those things on a regular basis. People sometimes don't catch on until they've heard about something five or ten times—then they respond. Don't let this become another ministry fad that fades away after a few months.

TRUTH FROM THE TRENCHES

Communicate your vision for parents and families to your congregation. Keep talking about it and find ways to give it visibility in the church. It will take more than a single pre-

Invite parents to take part

Begin making direct contact with parents and invite them to get involved in the youth ministry. There are multiple opportunities and levels for involvement for parents to choose from. (We'll look at these in chapters 9 and 10.)

Build a leadership team

A ministry to and with parents requires teamwork. You'll want to identify a core group of parents who can take on leadership roles (things like recruiting other parents, leading a parents' support group, and more). Find someone who will serve as your point person; if you want your partnership to prosper, you'll need to find someone who will help keep it on the front burner and maintain momentum. (You may not be able to do that even though you have a passion for it.) Give the person you're designating as your point an obvious and respected title, like Coordinator of Parent Ministries. It's then clear to everyone else who they should contact when they have special needs and requests. You may not find anyone with much experience because this is a relatively new concept in youth ministry. But you should invest in that person by sending him or her to ministry conferences and training events that have an emphasis on family-based youth ministry. (For more on building great teams, see one of the companion books in this series, *Building & Mobilizing Teams*, by Marv Penner.)

GET YOUR EFFORT GOING, LEARN FROM YOUR MISTAKES, AND KEEP TRYING

After you've done all your soil prep, planting, and cultivating, you can start trying some things and reaping the harvest. There are plenty of ideas to choose from in part three of this book. Again, you don't need to do everything at once—just do some things.

If you've ever planted a vegetable garden, you know that not everything is going to turn out all that great. As an amateur farmer, I've learned that despite my best efforts there will always be rotten tomatoes, bug-infested corn, and plenty of weeds. Not everything you try is going to succeed. Don't be surprised when all those parents who asked for a parent seminar don't show up when you actually schedule it because there was a playoff game on TV or a garage that needed to be cleaned. Don't be discouraged when you find that few people paid any attention to that cool newsletter you spent all day writing. Don't give up when parents seem disinterested or unresponsive. Give them—and anything you try—some time.

The important thing is that you stay the course and keep doing all you can to help parents and families succeed. It's really about doing what we know God has called us to do. Again, the Bible makes clear that the home is where faith is nurtured and passed on from one generation to the next, and we know that most families are not doing a very good job of that. George Barna reports that less than 10 percent of churchgoing families pray together (other than mealtimes) or join together in acts of service.[23] So we really shouldn't be surprised when parents don't respond like we think they should. A partnership with parents won't be easy or suddenly successful. It will be frustrating and at times very difficult. But like most worthwhile ministry endeavors, our calling is not to be successful; it's to be faithful. If we stay the course and keep on doing what we know are the right things, we can have faith that God will bless our efforts and give us a good harvest in due time. "Let us not become weary in doing good, for at the proper time we will reap a harvest if we do not give up" (Galatians 6:9).

ACTION PLAN

★ What are your long-term objectives and short-term action steps for involving parents in the youth ministry? Meet with some colleagues, the ministry staff at your church, or your leadership team and review those goals.

PUTTING TOGETHER A PLAN FOR PARENTS

★ How does a partnership with parents differ from simply adding programs for parents?

★ Chapter 4 laid out a number of potential obstacles that discourage youth workers from partnering with parents. Which of these—or any others—create discouragement in you?

★ What are you doing to be the spiritual leader in your own home?

★ Do you think it's possible to implement an effective ministry to and with parents without the support of the senior pastor and/or other church leaders? Why or why not?

★ What's the mission statement for your youth ministry? Does it include parents?

PART THREE

MAKING IT WORK

MAKING IT WORK BY BLESSING PARENTS

YOU MIGHT BE THE PARENT OF A TEENAGER IF . . .

★ Your friends and relatives no longer invite your family over for dinner.

★ Your teen's room decor can best be described as early landfill.

★ The clothes you bought for your kids just last month no longer fit or are somehow, suddenly no longer in style.

★ You text-message your teen in the next room to call her to dinner.

★ Your teen knows the lyrics to five hundred different songs but can't seem to remember what you told him ten minutes ago.

★ The TV remote that's been missing for a month finally appears in a pile of dirty laundry under your teen's bed.

★ After your teen takes a shower, there's not a drop of hot water left in the house.

★ Your teen asks you to drop her off two full blocks away from the school.

★ Your latest phone bill has unexplained calls totaling four thousand dollars.

★ You can no longer lift your teenager's backpack.

★ Your teen swears he knows more about the facts of life than you do.

★ Your car insurance policy—which you've had for twenty-five years—was just cancelled.

★ The door on your refrigerator is open more than it's shut.

★ Frozen pizza is on the menu five nights a week.

★ Your kids' allowance goes straight to purchasing music on iTunes.

★ The only time you seem to get any respect from your children is when you're adding minutes to their cell phone.

★ You start sounding like your parents!

One thing's for sure: if you're the parent of a teenager, you've probably heard plenty of jokes to remind you of your plight. Like this one: "When a child turns thirteen, you should put him in a pickle barrel, nail the lid shut, and feed him through a knothole. Then, when he turns sixteen, plug up the knothole." Mark Twain is most often credited for that one.

Most parents of teens at least try to keep their sense of humor. But sometimes raising teenagers is not very funny. Behind all the punch lines, what parents hear is a much scarier message: "Just wait until your kid hits puberty. She'll go into her bedroom, lock the door, and not come out for a month. When she finally does, you'll discover that your beautiful child has turned into an uncontrollable monster that will wreak havoc on your home and family for years to come. You're life is basically over!"

This is what has been called the myth of the teenage werewolf—and it strikes fear in the hearts of parents. When it is believed, it can also lead to discouragement and dysfunction in the home. Myths and stereotypes about parenting teenagers have a way of turning into self-fulfilling prophecies.

For that reason, I begin part three of this book with some ways to bring a little sunshine into the lives of parents—to be a blessing and an encouragement to them. With all the bad news parents hear about teens, we can be the people who bring good news. With all the discouragement they feel about how their kids are doing, we can bring encouragement. With all the criticism they get from their kids, we can bring a little affirmation. That's what this chapter is all about. When we bless parents, we not only lift their spirits, we also validate the important role they play in the lives of their kids. We can be cheerleaders for parents—people who believe in them and want the best for them and their kids.

HOW TO BLESS PARENTS

On the pages that follow, I'll give a list of ideas and suggestions for blessing parents. First, a word about the word *blessing*: in one sense, it's an older expression (in common use since sometime before the twelfth century!) but one that's come in style again. In its simplest form, it means something quite uncomplicated: to provide approval or encouragement. And that's exactly what you can do for parents.

Some of the blessings that follow involve programs and activities, but many do not. Most have to do with our attitude toward parents and the understanding that everything we do communicates volumes to kids and to parents as well.

Not long ago I conducted a survey of several thousand parents of teenagers from churches all around the country. I asked this question: "How has the youth ministry (or the youth leaders of your church) been a blessing to you and your family?" Not surprisingly, most of their responses had little to do with programs. They had more to do with the character and behavior of the youth leaders they've known and the casual encounters they've had with them. Many of my suggestions here are based on those responses from parents.

TRUTH FROM THE TRENCHES

You can be a cheerleader for parents—a consistent voice in their lives that believes in them and wants the best for them and their kids.

Be someone they want their kids to be around

As one parent put it: "The best thing a youth leader can do for me is to be a faithful follower of Jesus. It's so good to know that my kids have someone I can trust to be a positive role model for them."

Obviously, this one is not about programs; it's about you. The best way to bless parents is to guard your heart and give your own relationship with God first priority. Teens are not the only ones who are disappointed and disillusioned by the significant adults in their lives who fail in their integrity or moral purity. Parents are even more concerned. If you're not willing to be a role model for kids to follow, get out of youth ministry now. All this doesn't mean you have to be perfect, of course. It only means that you're taking seriously the responsibility given to you to set an example for kids and that you're living your life in a manner that is worthy of your calling.

Provide a place of safety for their kids

Safety showed up strong in the responses I got from parents about how youth workers can bless their lives. And it makes a lot of sense. As one mom put it: "I am grateful to our youth leaders for providing my daughter with a safe place to go. I am confident that she is always well supervised and surrounded by good people."

Parents are chronic worriers anyway, so there's no good reason to make them worry more when their kids are with us. We want kids to have a good time; parents want their kids to be safe. We worry about how many kids will show up for our events; parents worry about how many kids come home alive.

An example: for the past fifteen years we've taken our middle school youth group to Mexico for a mission trip. It's always a great week of ministry and literally life-changing for many of the kids who go. It's my favorite week of the year. But recently there's been a wave of violence across the Mexican border that has received a good deal of publicity in the news for several months. Word is out—at the time of this writing—that it's not safe for tourists in certain parts of Mexico right now.

If it were left just to me, I think we would just go ahead with plans for this year's mission trip to Mexico. The violence is not widespread and it rarely affects groups of people who are traveling together. But this decision is not left just to me. Many parents expressed fears about their kids traveling in Mexico and so we changed our plans. I understand the need to encourage students (and parents) to take risks and to get out of their comfort zones. But this was not a battle worth fighting. There are other, safer ways to accomplish the same ministry goals and we can save our risk-taking for another day.

Parents need assurance that we're doing all we can to provide safe environments for their kids. That's why it's important to do background checks on all your volunteer leaders and require their attendance at training seminars. Let parents know that they can trust the adults who are coming in contact with their kids. Safety-check all vehicles that are used to transport your youth and make sure the drivers are licensed, insured, and qualified to drive. Screen all games and activities for potential hazards that might cause physical injury or undue embarrassment. I can tell you from experience that some good ideas are just not worth the harm that can potentially be done to kids. Obviously, not everything is under our control and accidents do happen, but there are precautions we can take to provide great experiences for kids without putting them in harm's way. Remember, we're stewards of young people who do not belong to us.[24]

Be a cheerleader for kids

Parents don't really need to hear more bad news about teenagers. There's plenty of that everywhere they turn. If you want to bless parents, provide them with good news about kids (especially their kids) from time to time. Be bullish on teenagers! One parent said: "Our youth minister loves teenagers and that's such an encouragement to me. His enthusiasm for kids is contagious."

I have never been fond of scaring parents with statements like "Every day in America, 1,295 teenagers run away from home." I don't know who comes up with statistics like these but, based on the fact that there are more than 35 million teenagers in America, I think we can safely say that most teenagers (maybe 34.99 million or so) don't run away from their homes. In fact, they like being at home and actually like having their parents around the house! That's what parents need to hear.

I'm not saying we should stick our heads in the sand and ignore some of the very real struggles that our teens face every day. No one can deny that many kids are having a tough time growing up. But adolescence is not an illness. Parents and other adults need to know that we have not given up on today's teenagers. Our kids will be just fine if we pay attention to them and give them plenty of encouragement.

Communicate your vision clearly

You can bless parents by having a clear vision of youth ministry and communicating it to parents with regularity. Parents need to know what you're trying to accomplish, what your goals and objectives are. Once they know those, they'll be more likely to support you and pray for you because they'll know what to pray for.

Get organized

I know, it's not your spiritual gift. But nothing irks parents more than having to deal with a youth worker's failure to plan events properly or to communicate what's going on. The more competent you appear to be as a leader, the more trust you'll get from parents and the more you'll bless them. One parent said: "I don't know how our youth pastor gets everything done, but he does. We have confidence in his ability to be a spiritual leader for our kids."

Don't think you have what it takes? Sign up for a time management course or read a good book on leadership. Anyone can get more organized (it's a skill, not a spiritual gift) if they want to. Meanwhile, find someone who is organized and make them part of your leadership team. Parents will love you for it.

Respect and reinforce family values

Be careful not to undermine the values that parents hold or the tough decisions they sometimes have to make at home. For example, if you have kids in your youth group who are not allowed to view certain kinds of movies or listen to certain kinds of music or participate in certain kinds of activities, avoid violating their family values in your youth ministry. Just as important: avoid criticizing their parents or characterizing them as being too strict or old-fashioned. Over the years I've come to appreciate—and applaud—parents who are willing to set limits and provide discipline for their children, even when those limits might be a little bit over the top.

I realize that you can't please all the parents all the time, but it's wise to pick your battles wisely in youth ministry. If you want to get (and keep) parents on your team, don't throw away your relationship with them (or throw away your job) over stuff that really doesn't matter. Make sure you have a good understanding of what the boundaries are with the parents in your group; stay within them to the best of your ability. Parents will be blessed when they know they can trust you to support them and respect their authority.

TRUTH FROM THE TRENCHES

Be careful not to undermine the values that parents hold or the tough decisions they sometimes have to make at home. Always avoid criticizing parents or characterizing them as being too strict or old-fashioned.

Pay attention to their kids

In my survey with parents, several of them wrote, "The youth pastor (or leader) has really made my (son/daughter) feel included and special." Parents are blessed when they know that their kids are getting attention. We also want every kid to feel included, to feel special, to feel like they're wanted and needed. One parent wrote: "Our youth minister believes in really getting to know every kid in the youth group and building a relationship with them. In return, they trust him, believe what he tells them about Jesus, and they want to be involved."

Obviously, there are limitations here. Not even the best youth workers can get to know more than a few kids at a time. If your group is large, you'll want to make sure you have a team of adults that's spending time with your teens and making sure they all feel fully accepted. This single action alone blesses parents in immense ways.

Brag on their kids

When my own children were teens, I'm embarrassed to say, I was often surprised when someone would tell me they liked them. I actually wondered if they didn't have my kids confused with somebody else's! But it always felt great to get compliments about my children. Looking back, I realize that I was probably so focused on my kids' shortcomings that I didn't notice how well they were doing, which was usually much better than I thought.

I've since discovered that this is true for almost all parents. One of the best gifts you can give a parent is to say something encouraging about their kids. Parents are starved for a few positive indicators that their children are going to be OK. Not only can we bless parents by bragging on their teens, we can give them hope! This is especially true for parents whose kids aren't doing so well.

Make a habit, especially, of noting those positive character traits in your teens that you can attribute directly to their parents. For example, if one of your students has been helpful, call his parents or drop them a quick note. Say something like: "Hey, I just wanted to let you know that Sean has been a great help to me the last couple of weeks. He has a real servant's heart, which I know he got from you. Thanks for doing such a great job with him." Needless to say, comments like those will make the buttons pop off the shirt of every parent who hears them.

Brag on parents to their kids

Make a habit of letting your teens know that you hold their parents in high esteem. When you're having conversations with your students, show an interest in their parents and, if you can, say something positive like "Your parents seem pretty cool. . . . Do you think they'd like to come along on one of our mission trips?" Or "Whenever I talk to your parents, they always seem so proud of you." Or "Hey, when are you going to introduce me to your dad?" Just as parents sometimes have a distorted view of their kids, so teens sometimes have a hard time believing their parents are cool.

Honor Parents of the Week

Along the same lines, here's a program idea that can really bless parents (and their teens as well). Each week—or once a month, depending on the size of your group—have your teens nominate their folks to be Parents of the Week. Select parents from those nominations and then honor them at one of your youth group meetings. You can either have them come in person or you can create a short video featuring the parents in their normal environment. Or do both! Have the kids introduce their parents to the youth group and brag on them a bit. Then present them with a nice gift basket or an award or certificate that designates them as Parents of the Week.

If you fear this might get a bit too competitive in your ministry, there are variations. Two ideas are to honor parents on their wedding anniversaries (give them flowers and a card from the group) or on their birthdays.

Do try this at home

Put a family spin on all your teaching. Any lesson that you teach from Scripture can be applied to life at home. If you're teaching on the subject of worship, you can ask kids, "How do you worship God at home?" If you're teaching on love: "How can you show love to members of your own family?" Regardless of the topic, you can ask questions like these:

★   What are some ways you can put this into practice at home this week?
★   How do you think this will impact the relationship you have with your parents?
★   How do you think your parents would answer this question?

Always give teens specific suggestions on how to apply what you're teaching to their family life. They need to know that unless our faith is being put into practice at home first, we can't really put it into practice anywhere else. (For that matter, adults need to know this as well!) Parents will be blessed when they can see the faith of their children being lived out at home.

Put honey on the Torah

There is an ancient Hebrew tradition of dripping honey on a child's slate in which words from the Torah (the body of wisdom and law in Jewish literature, most commonly thought of as the first five books of the Old Testament) are being studied. The children were encouraged to literally lick the honey off the slate that contained the holy words, in this way associating the sweetness of the honey with the sweetness of God's Word.[25]

Actually, that sounds a lot like what most of us do in our youth group programming—we try to create engaging programs for students that draw them to the Word of God. Parents hate having to force or drag their kids to church with them. In my surveys with parents, the quality of the youth group programs ranked very high: "I'm so thankful that my son enjoys attending our church's youth activities. That has been a real blessing to our family."

In my church, our middle school and high school groups meet on Sunday mornings during the church's first worship service. Students are then encouraged to attend the second worship service with their parents in the big house (sanctuary). While age-appropriate teaching and worship is a feature of these youth meetings, they're not intended to be a church substitute for teenagers. They are "honey on the Torah" that draws teens to the church and to the people who are there to serve them. When we strive for excellence in our youth ministry programming, we bless parents and families.

Have an open-door policy

You can bless parents by regularly communicating to them that they're welcome to attend any youth group meeting or activity at any time. They don't have to do anything except hang out, observe what's going on, and maybe say hi to some kids. They may not take advantage of your offer very often, but it's an encouragement for parents to know that they have an open invitation to the youth group anytime they choose.

Set up a Random Acts of Kindness Team

Put together a Random Acts of Kindness team in your youth ministry. Have it made up of students who plan and execute "attacks" on selected parents throughout the year. These attacks can include such things as secretly "flowering" their house—either by planting flowers in their yard or bringing them a bouquet of cut flowers—washing their cars, mowing the lawn, washing windows, or performing some other act of service that expresses kindness and gratitude.

Not quite so random is, as mentioned before, to remember special days like a couple's wedding anniversary, a birthday, or Valentine's Day. A card from the youth group or special act of kindness on these days can be a great way to bless parents and also to encourage students to honor their parents.

Pray for parents

Make a commitment to pray for parents on a regular basis. We often ask parents to pray for the youth ministry and for us, but it's equally important and beneficial that we pray for them. They are the most important spiritual influence on their kids and we should hold them up in prayer continually.

Here's an idea that might help: Get all the photos that you can of the parents, either from the students, the parents, or by taking photos yourself. Then create parent prayer cards with those photos; the cards can serve as a visual aid for you and other members of your ministry team as you pray for parents each week, rotating through the stack of cards and praying for a few each time. You can also use these cards to record prayer requests from those families as you receive them. Periodically, let parents know that you're praying for them— they'll be blessed and encouraged.

TRUTH FROM THE TRENCHES

Make a commitment to pray for the parents of your students on a regular basis. We often ask parents to pray for the youth ministry and for us, but it's equally important and beneficial that we pray for them.

Have your students pray for their parents

Take time during your youth group meetings to pray for parents. Veteran youth worker and author Marv Penner has created a special prayer tool for students that can be used in a group setting.[26] Lead your students through the following prayer. Ask them to think of their parents (or guardians) while you slowly pray through each letter of the word **PARENT:**

P – Pressure: Identify a specific pressure that your mom or dad is experiencing right now. It could be job pressure, money pressure, or a health problem. Pray that your mom and dad will be able to handle it and become stronger as a result.

A –Attitude: Ask God to help you with any attitudes toward your parents.

R – Relationship: What relationships do your parents have that need prayer? How can you improve the relationship you have with your parents?

E – Emotions: What emotions have you noticed in your parents that need prayer? Maybe they've felt fear, anger, worry, sadness, depression . . . pray that God will give them hope and healing from negative emotions.

N –Needs: What special needs do your parents have?

T – Thanks: Thank God for your parents, no matter how imperfect they may be.

This guide also can be printed on wallet-sized cards so your students can pray for their parents on their own.

Send birthday congratulation cards

For a unique way to bless parents, send them a congratulations card on the event of their teen's birthday. You may need to create custom cards yourself since they may be hard to find at a local store. Here's some sample copy:

"On the event of your child's birthday . . .
Hey, thanks for bringing   (name here)   into the world. She/he is such a
blessing to all of us. She/he is growing in great ways in _____. It's a joy to
have _____ in the ministry."

Teach the Fifth Commandment

The only commandment specifically directed to children and young people, which also comes with a promise, is the fifth: "Honor your father and your mother, so that you may live long in the land" (Exodus 20:12). It's actually the first commandment dealing with interpersonal relationships. All the others—about lying, stealing, murder, and more—follow this one.

It only makes sense, then, that we take time to teach the Fifth Commandment in positive and practical terms to our kids. You don't have to be heavy-handed or one-sided in your teaching. Students can be taught that keeping this commandment has huge benefits for them as well as their parents. I've written a book for students, *Read This Book or You're Grounded*, which helps students understand, honor, and communicate with their parents. The book, which has a student curriculum piece along with it, is a series of lessons for teens on this subject.[27]

Hold Mother's and Father's Day banquets

Here's another fun event students can put on for their parents. On your calendar, find the day that falls exactly halfway between Mother's Day and Father's Day (the day of the week will vary from year to year). Plan a banquet or some other special event for parents on this day; honor all the moms and dads. If possible, let the kids do the planning and promotion, cook the meal, serve the food, and provide the entertainment. Guaranteed: parents will absolutely love this one.

Help parents out on Valentine's Day

Let's return to the idea of doing something special for Valentine's Day. Sometimes parents, especially dads, don't really know what to do on that night anyway. So why not plan an evening out for them that focuses on kids expressing love to their parents? As cheesy as something like this may sound, parents always love it when their kids do something nice for them. Don't forget—whenever you plan an event involving parents, make sure you plan it far enough in advance to get it on everybody's calendars.

But here's a possibly even better option for Valentine's Day: set up a free baby-sitting service for the holiday so parents can have a romantic evening out. Perhaps the youth group can provide roses for the moms as well.

Attend special family events

You can bless parents by showing up for special family events when you're invited or when they're open to the public. When a student in your group is performing in a play, giving a recital, playing in an athletic event, having a birthday party, receiving an award, graduating from high school . . . these are all special times for kids and families. It means a lot to parents when you share it with them and show support.

Take lots of pictures

Parents love to get photos of their kids. Take lots of pictures or videos of youth group activities and copy them to parents. If you have someone in your group who is skilled at video editing and production, have them take this on as a ministry.

Make your teens visible

If it's possible, find ways for your teenagers to be involved in the regular adult worship services of the church. Perhaps they can read Scripture, usher, provide special music, or participate in some other way. Parents love to see their kids in a positive light. The occasional youth-led service can bless parents as well as the whole church. Another idea: if your church uses PowerPoint or some other presentation software for pre-church announcements, include photos or videos of youth group activities from time to time.

Use frequent words of encouragement

Make a habit of calling parents or sending them personal notes by mail or e-mail or text message. It always blesses them to receive simple words of encouragement like:

- ★ I really appreciate your support.
- ★ Your kids are amazing.
- ★ I prayed for your family today.
- ★ You're doing a great job with your (son/daughter).
- ★ You are such an encouragement to me.
- ★ Thanks for being such a great example for other parents.
- ★ Thanks for your willingness to get involved.
- ★ I really enjoy having your (son/daughter) in our group.
- ★ When my kids get older, I hope they turn out as great as yours did!

Of course, the more personal you can make these notes, the better. Try to mention specific things when you can, such as: "(Teen's name) mentioned to me the accident you had at work last week. I hope you're feeling better by now and I want you to know that I'm praying for you." Or "Thanks for the helpful suggestion you made at our last parent meeting about the music. I've put someone in charge of listening carefully to everything we play at our youth meetings from now on. We'll make sure it's decent for our kids to listen to! I appreciate your willingness to speak up!"

ACTION PLAN

★ Which of the ideas in this chapter that you're not doing can you put in place right away? Which might take a few months but could be put in place within a year? Be determined to start somewhere.

MAKING IT WORK BY COMMUNICATING WITH PARENTS

"Hey Mom, I'm going out tonight. It's our youth group thing."

"What?"

"You remember, I told you. It's our youth group thing."

"No, I don't remember. *What* youth group thing?"

"All the kids in the youth group are going."

"What I want to know is *what* are you going *to*? What will you be doing?"

"Mom, our youth pastor said it's going to be a RIOT—which stands for REALLY-INTENSE-OVER-THE-TOP, or something like that. I'm not sure what it is."

"And where is this RIOT?"

"Um, at a hotel or conference center or something. We're meeting at the church and everybody's riding together. Oh, and it costs thirty-five dollars. But I'll need forty. We might stop for snacks on the way home."

"Forty dollars? You've got to be kidding."

"I told you about this last week!!"

"You didn't tell me anything about forty dollars."

"Well, I can't remember to tell you *everything*. Why do you always have to be so lame!"

"I don't think you're going anywhere tonight, young lady."

"MOM! IT'S JUST A YOUTH GROUP THING!!"

Some of our best ideas in youth ministry can blow up on us big time if we don't communicate well with parents. If you truly want to engage parents and make them partners in your youth ministry, you'll want to make sure they're in the information loop on everything you do. Conversations like the one above should never happen. Even worse, you don't want that parent to come knocking on your door or the door of your senior pastor demanding information that you easily could have provided.

Remember that the best communication goes both ways. It involves both talking and listening. We need to talk to parents and keep them informed of everything we're doing, but we also need to listen to them and take their input seriously. When we do that, we demonstrate respect, humility, and transparency—all essential qualities for effective youth ministry.

In my surveys with parents, I received this comment from the parent of a teen: "One of the biggest blessings we receive from our youth ministry is that we have an open line of communication with our youth minister. He is not afraid to talk with parents and is open to ideas and suggestions from any parent. Whenever we talk to him about our child or something within the ministry, he is 'quick to listen and slow to speak.' . . . To be heard, understood, and loved through our youth ministry is the biggest blessing that, I believe, any parent would appreciate."

Take note of this: Everyone should be quick to listen, slow to speak and slow to become angry, for man's anger does not bring about the righteous life that God desires.

JAMES 1: 19, 20

FIND OUT WHO THEY ARE

It almost goes without saying that the first step toward good communication is to know whom you're communicating with. I can't tell you how many envelopes I've received over the years addressed "To the parents of Nathan/Amber/Corey Rice." My initial reaction to such mail is to assume that if I'm not important enough for the sender to learn my name, then what's inside the envelope probably isn't important enough for me to read.

If you want parents to take your communication with them seriously, learn their names and a few other important facts about them as well. You can do this with a personal interview or you can gather information through a parent survey like the one at the end of this chapter.

And again, remember that this kind of getting acquainted should go both ways. I recommend that you put together a complete bio on yourself and other members of your youth ministry leadership team and provide them to each parent, along with any other information you want them to have. They shouldn't have to guess or worry about who's hanging out with their kids at the church.

TRUTH FROM THE TRENCHES

If you want parents to take your communication seriously, learn their names and a few other important facts about them as well. You can do this with a personal interview or you can gather information through a parent survey.

BIG BENEFITS

Besides the obvious practical benefits of communication—such as the little details like, uh, letting parents know when to pick up their kids— good communication provides the grease that keeps the wheels of our parent-partnership effort turning smoothly and efficiently.

Remember that when you communicate well with parents you keep them engaged and feeling more like they're part of your team. And that's your goal. By doing this simple thing, parents will have a better understanding of what you're doing and they'll be advocates for you with the rest of the church. It's not uncommon for people to talk about what's going on in the church and, quite often, they don't know what they're talking about. Rumors and other misinformation can be corrected or explained by parents who have an inside track and some ownership in the youth ministry.

Effective communication is also a good way to get helpful feedback on what you're doing. If you make a habit of communicating your plans early in the process, you'll save yourself lots of headaches later on. I can remember many times planning events on dates that looked clear on the church calendar—but weren't clear on too many family calendars. The early involvement of parents helps you avoid mistakes like that.

Communicating early and often is also a great way to invite parents to be part of what you're doing. Remember that parents rarely say no to everything. Just because they turned you down once doesn't mean they won't say yes next time. Keep on contacting them and letting them know about upcoming opportunities to get involved. Eventually, they will.

A FEW COMMUNICATION TIPS

If you want to avoid serious communication breakdowns with parents, keep these tips in mind:

★ Early communication is better communication. Families are extremely busy these days, so the earlier you can let people know what's going on, the happier you're going to make them. If you want a good turnout for anything that involves parents, get it on your calendar—and theirs—at least six months in advance. For camps and mission trips, a year in advance isn't too early to start talking about even the earliest of plans.

★ Don't communicate to parents through their kids. Sometimes we assume parents know what's going on because we made an announcement at youth group and specifically told students, "Now be sure to tell your parents . . . " Or we give kids a printed handout with all the information right there in black and white and expect them to take it home and give it to their parents. Sometimes we even think we can send personal messages to parents through their kids: "Tell your dad thanks for loaning us his SUV last week! And be sure to tell him I'm real sorry about the broken windshield." Guess what? Those types of messages usually get stuck somewhere in the frontal lobe of a teenager's brain and never see the light of day—and wouldn't be appreciated anyway. Bottom line: If you want to communicate with parents, communicate directly with them, not through their kids.

★ If you send e-mail announcements to students, copy them to parents as well.

★ Communicate in the language of parents. Remember that communicating with kids is very different from communicating with parents. That very cool flyer with the latest edgy graphics and unreadable fonts? Probably won't grab the attention of parents. They'll just assume it's not for them. If you use printed materials or design a Web site, make sure it passes muster with parents who speak the language of fortysomethings.

★ Along the same lines, avoid sloppy, unprofessional communication. Proofread your printed materials to eliminate the kinds of mistakes that reflect badly on you and the ministry.

★ If you have a large number of parents to communicate with, divide and conquer. Recruit a team of parents or other volunteers to whom you can delegate some of the communication. This, of course, requires some leadership skills on your part and you'll need to make sure your volunteers have the expertise, training, and constant support they need to do this job effectively.

★ Avoid overcommunication. Don't spam parents with unnecessary e-mail that forces them to sort out meaningful communication from the rest of the junk they get every day in their e-mail box.

★ Keep it personal. Yep, I've mentioned this already, but it's worth repeating. Learn the names of the parents of your teens and address your communication to them personally, not to "Dear Parent."

TRUTH FROM THE TRENCHES

If you want to communicate with parents, communicate directly with them, not through their kids.

WHAT TO COMMUNICATE

Keep in mind that parents are probably going to be interested in details that kids really don't care that much about. Here is some of the information you'll want to make sure parents know about any youth ministry activity that you have planned:

★   What exactly will happen at this event? What is the program?

★   When is it? What's the date, what time does it start, and when does it end?

★   Why are you doing this event? What's the purpose behind it and what do you hope to accomplish?

★   Who is going to be there? What age groups are invited? How many adults will be there? Who's in charge? Am I invited? Can my child invite others to go?

★   Where is it? If it involves travel, where do the kids meet and how do you get there? Who's driving? What vehicles will be used? What route will you take? Will there be stops along the way? Where will you end up?

★   What are the costs? Besides the obvious ones, are there any hidden costs like snacks, souvenirs, offerings?

★   How do I get more information? Is there an emergency contact number or a Web site that has more info?

You may not need to provide all of this information on every single event, but know for sure that parents want all these details, and probably more, for many of your activities. Make sure you've made every effort to communicate all the details to parents in an effective and easy-to-access way.

Here are more good ideas for communicating with parents.

Parent newsletters

As long as there have been copy machines (and they've been around a pretty long time), there have been parent newsletters. The trick is to be consistent with them (make them monthly or quarterly) and make them interesting enough that parents will actually read them.

E-mail newsletters are growing in popularity because they are easy and inexpensive to produce, but they sometimes fail to have the impact that a good old-fashioned paper-and-ink newsletter can have. My recommendation is to publish a printed newsletter once a quarter and send out e-mail blasts on a more frequent (monthly or semi-monthly) schedule.

Effective parent newsletters don't have to be fancy, although if you or someone you know has the time and talent to create an elaborately designed publication with lots of snazzy graphics and photos, go for it. There are some great computer programs that make composing professional-looking newsletters much easier. But again, the important thing is to focus on the *content* so that parents will read it.

If you're including a calendar of events in your newsletter, let me suggest that you publish all of the new or changed events highlighted in red. This will allow parents to note all the changes and additions without having to read through the entire calendar each time it's published.

You can also create interest by including photos and short articles by students and staff members. Specific articles for parents, such as articles dealing with youth culture or parenting issues, are also effective.

There are some excellent parent newsletters available from organizations like HomeWord (www.homeword.com), Youth Specialties (www.youthspecialties.com), and Group Publishing (www.youthministry.com); you can e-mail (simply forward) these to parents or glean information from these while crediting them as the resource. Another great resource on youth culture trends is the Center for Parent/Youth Understanding (www.cpyu.org).

Parents' Web page

If your youth ministry has a Web site, create a page that's specifically targeted to parents. Provide plenty of information about your youth ministry and links to other Web sites of interest. Make it easy for parents to get the information they need quickly and accurately. Be sure to keep it updated; simply make this a checklist item that you get to every week.

Youth group hot line

It doesn't really cost that much to have a dedicated phone line that parents can call at any time and get the information they need. They shouldn't have to call the church and work their way through a maze of options to find out what time the kids need to be at the church or what they need to bring for your next outing.

Youth ministry on display

Does your church have a lobby or coffee house or some common area where people hang out before, between, or after worship services? Why not put up a display or booth that promotes the youth ministry? Provide flyers and photos, and have someone who's knowledgeable about upcoming events and programs work the booth. Yes, it's another detail to worry about, but sometimes you can find a parent who's willing to take charge of something like this.

Youth ministry Web cam

If you have someone on your team with enough tech know-how, add streaming video to your youth ministry's Web site. This can give parents a peek at selected youth activities when they're unable to attend in person.

The house phone

Here's a little one that's a gem but easy to overlook: when you call one of your students in the youth group, call the house phone. If a parent answers, don't ask for the student right away. Talk to the parent for a while.

Snail mail

It still works. In fact, using the regular postal service is working better than ever now that postage has gone up and so many advertisers are using e-mail. Hard copy mail gets a little more attention. Just keep it short and sweet. Postcards are ideal. If you want parents to read your mail and not toss it, make sure you address it to them personally (have I mentioned this one before?).

Youth ministry open house

A great way to introduce yourself, your ministry team, and the youth ministry program to parents is to hold an annual open house just like most schools do. Put on a typical youth group meeting and have the parents participate as if they were teens themselves. This is always a good idea early in the school year. It's a great way to meet parents and let them know your mission and goals for the year. You can also let parents know what you're going to be teaching or focusing on during the year so they can reinforce these messages at home.

Home visits

Make it a priority to visit the home of every student in your youth ministry. Every social worker knows how essential it is to visit a client's home; the same should be true in youth ministry. I know one youth pastor who printed the line "Available most nights of the week for dinner" under his name on his business card. He got a few free meals and also a chance to meet parents and visit the home environment of some of the students in the ministry.

Parent permission slips

Use them frequently if for no other reason than to let parents know exactly what's going on. It's not uncommon for parents to have the wrong information about youth events, and a parent permission slip can clear away a lot of the fog.

Parent survey

To get some basic information on each parent, ask them to fill out a survey once a year (or update their previous one annually). You can use the survey below, or one similar to it. You might also ask parents to provide you with a family picture (like the one many families send out at Christmas), or perhaps you can take one. Use this information to help you get better acquainted with parents; learn how, or how much, they would like to be involved; and to better understand the needs of students and their families.

Name: ....

Married? ❏ yes ❏ no

If yes, spouse's name?...................................

Number of years married?...............................

Address: ....

....

Phone numbers (home, cell, work):...............

....

E-mail address:...

Emergency contact number:.........................

Your occupation:.......................................

Children's names, ages, where they attend school: ....

....

....

Blended family? ❏ yes ❏ no

Do you attend (name of your church)? ❏ yes ❏ no

If yes, how long have you been attending? Are you a member?

....

If no, do you attend another church? What is your religious background? ....

How can the youth ministry serve you and your children? ....

Do you or your children have special needs we should be aware of? ....

Would you be willing to attend activities or special events designed for parents of teens?

....

Would you be willing to serve as a youth ministry volunteer from time to time?...............

Parent surveys, part two

In addition to the annual parent survey, give parents other opportunities to provide you with feedback on a regular basis. You can send out printed surveys or use a Web service like www.SurveyMonkey.com to create questionnaires on any topic. And sometimes it's fun to have both your teens and their parents take the same survey and then compare results.

ACTION PLAN

★ Go back over the many ways to communicate with parents listed in this chapter. Which are you doing well? Which can you do better? Which can you add?

MAKING IT WORK BY EQUIPPING PARENTS

Parents will be much more likely to partner with the youth ministry if they know that the youth ministry exists to serve them just as much as it exists to serve their kids.

It's safe to say that most of the programming we do in the church is age-segregated. There are programs and activities for the kids, there are programs and activities for the teens, and of course the same things exist for the adults. But real life isn't divided up that way. Parents and teenagers live together in the same house, interact with each other daily, and the relationship they have with each other impacts their lives for years to come. In fact, most of life is lived together in families. But the reality is that few parents and teens are equipped to do this successfully—and few churches offer much help.

You've heard it before: neither children nor teens come with instruction manuals (which really hasn't been a problem until the last generation or two). Parents of the past learned how to parent from their parents. But today, grandma and grandpa may live in a retirement village, and most parents are on their own. They feel isolated, alone, and ill-equipped to meet the challenges of raising teenagers in today's world.

That's why it's important for youth ministries to come alongside parents with the help they need. This chapter offers a number of ideas for equipping parents to be better parents and to help them pass their faith on to their kids.

TRUTH FROM THE TRENCHES

Parents will be much more likely to partner with the youth ministry if they know that the youth ministry exists to serve them just as much as it exists to serve their kids.

Remember that if you're not a parent yourself and lack the training or experience to offer parenting advice, *you* will want to take advantage of the many resources and people available in this area. But at the same time remember that you don't have to become a parenting expert to help equip parents.

PARENT SEMINARS, CLASSES, AND WORKSHOPS

Almost twenty-five years ago, researchers Merton Strommen and A. Irene Strommen surveyed thousands of parents of teenagers and published their findings in a book called *Five Cries of Parents*.[28] The Strommens identified "The Cry for Understanding" as the number one felt need of parents. More than anything else, parents wanted to know what to expect during their children's teen years and how they could respond in positive ways. For the same reasons, I developed a seminar for parents around the same time. I called it Understanding Your Teenager. This seminar has been presented in hundreds of churches over the past twenty years and has helped thousands of parents. It continues to do so.

What was true a quarter-century ago is no less true today. Parents still struggle with their children because they lack understanding. Scripture says, "By wisdom a house is built, and through understanding it is established" (Proverbs 24:3). You can help parents gain wisdom and understanding by hosting or presenting parent seminars, classes, and workshops that will enlighten them and give them the tools they need to succeed at home. Seminars not only provide parents with information and ideas, they also encourage parents, connect them with other parents, and offer hope. Parent seminars on relevant topics can also be a great entry point for parents who haven't been part of your church or youth ministry.

I've found that the best seminars for parents need to be short and have a clear objective. Parents are extremely busy and don't have time to attend weekend retreats or all-day events. Some churches have had success with longer events, but it's necessary to plan them at least a year in advance in order to get them on everybody's calendar and to get a decent turnout. You'll get a better response if the seminar is no longer than three hours—taking up only part of the day—or an evening seminar.

Effective parent seminars also need to be positive. If you give your seminar a title like "Parenting Rebellious Teenagers" or "How to Get Your Teen Off Drugs," you'll have a poor turnout simply because many parents hate to admit (publicly anyway) that they are dealing with issues of this nature.

So keep it positive. Some of the seminars you might consider, like those held by Understanding Your Teenager, are available from organizations like HomeWord, Youth Specialties, or the Center for Parent/Youth Understanding (CPYU). You'll get a first-rate speaker and all of the seminar materials in a package deal. While most of these seminars are reasonably priced, they may be more expensive than your church can afford. If so, it's worth considering joining forces with several other churches in your area to cohost a seminar in a neutral location. Some of these seminars may also be available as a DVD-based curriculum that come with discussion guides and leader materials.

TRUTH FROM THE TRENCHES

I've found that the best seminars for parents need to be short and have a clear objective; parents are extremely busy. They also need to be positive. Don't give your workshop a title like "Parenting Rebellious Teenagers."

Here are just a few examples of seminar topics that can be helpful for the parents in your church:

★   Understanding Your Teenager
★   Understanding Today's Youth Culture
★   Generation 2 Generation: Passing the Baton of Faith on to Your Kids
★   Building Healthy Morals and Values: How to Help Your Kids Make Wise Choices in a Whatever World
★   Helping Your Teenager Succeed in School
★   The Straight Scoop on Sex and Relationships
★   Give Them Wings: Raising Capable Kids
★   Enjoy Your Middle Schooler
★   Serious Senioritis: Helping Your High Schooler Make a Smooth Transition to College or a Career
★   Traits of a Happy, Healthy Family

BEEN THERE, DONE THAT

An alternative to a parent seminar is to invite a "panel of experts" made up of members of your church who have raised their own children to adulthood and lived to tell about it! These parents don't have to be experts in any professional sense of the word or have to have model children; in fact, it's often helpful to have parents on such a panel who have experienced difficulties with their kids.

Prepare a list of questions (maybe even collect them from parents in your youth ministry) and give it to your panelists ahead of time. You can use the list to help publicize the event. When parents know what questions are going to be tackled, they'll be more likely to attend.

Here's a sample list:

★   What was the biggest challenge you faced as the parent of a teenager?
★   How did you handle your teen's expenses? Did you provide an allowance for them, provide a credit card, make them earn their own money?
★   Do you think it's easier to raise teenage boys or teenage girls? Why?
★   How did you handle the issue of chores and responsibilities with your teen?
★   What limits did you set for your teen regarding sex and dating? Or did you?
★   What did you do to prepare your teen for leaving home?
★   What kinds of consequences work best with teenagers?
★   What are some family traditions your teens enjoyed?
★   What did you do to help your teenager grow in his/her faith?
★   If you had it all to do over again, what would you do differently as a parent?

COUNSELING SERVICES/FAMILY COACHING

If there's a professional family counselor in your area, invite him or her to come to a parent meeting or class and field a few questions on parenting teenagers. You may need to pay him or her for their time, but this would be a great investment in families.

You can also provide parents with the names of counselors, treatment centers, and other resources in your community. Don't wait for them to come to you for help.

They probably won't because they may feel embarrassed or ashamed. In general, let parents know where they can get trustworthy help and guidance when they need it.

TEACH FAITH-BUILDING SKILLS

According to a great deal of research, many Christian parents don't know how to pray with their kids, how to read or study the Bible with their kids, how to lead their children to Christ, how to have faith conversations with their kids, or how to talk with them about issues like sex and drugs.

Why not take time on a regular basis to teach some of these faith-building skills to parents? The Bible says to "assemble the people . . . to hear my words so that they may learn to revere me" (Deuteronomy 4:10). We can do this by providing both the instruction and the tools for parents to communicate their faith to their kids.

Teach [God's decrees and laws] to your children and to their children after them. Remember the day you stood before the Lord your God at Horeb, when he said to me, "Assemble the people before me to hear my words so that they may learn to revere me as long as they live in the land and may teach them to their children."

D E U T E R O N O M Y 4 : 9 , 1 0

One simple way we can help parents initiate faith conversations with their teens is to provide them with "talk starters" or discussion questions they can use to carry out the lessons we've taught in our youth groups. Whenever you have a Bible study with students or challenge them with a new teaching, why not provide parents with some encouragement and guidance for discussing it with their teens? Not all parents will take advantage, but some will, and their teens will benefit greatly from the reinforcement your teaching gets at home. And that, in the truest sense, is what a parent-youth ministry partnership is all about.

A PARENT'S PLEDGE

This pledge form can be another effective way to develop a partnership between your youth ministry and the parents who are willing to come alongside:

"As for me and my household, we will serve the Lord."
JOSHUA 24:15

A PARENT'S PLEDGE

I (we), the parent(s) of _____ , pledge before God, and with the help and grace of God, to raise our children "in the training and instruction of the Lord" (Ephesians 6:4).

EXAMPLE: I will set a great example for my children by spending personal time in worship, Bible study, prayer, and service to Christ.

DEVOTIONS: I will read the Bible and pray with, or have a time of devotions with, my family at least once a week.

CONVERSATIONS: I will initiate conversations with my children about the Christian faith and how faith relates to everyday life.

FAMILY CULTURE: Our family will do things together (traditions, celebrations, other activities) that clearly identify us as Christ-followers.

CHURCH: Our family will attend church services together on a regular basis.

MINISTRY: Our family will be involved in ministries that serve others.

MENTORS: I will encourage my children to develop healthy relationships with caring Christian adults outside the home.

MEALTIMES: With exceptions only, our family will have a meal together—with the TV off—at least once a day.

ENCOURAGEMENT: I will give my children encouragement (a blessing of some type) every day.

PRAYER: I will pray for my children every day.

Signature: _____ Date: _____
Signature: _____ Date: _____

As the youth pastor of _____ church, I pledge before God to support you as you seek to live faithfully for Christ in your home. I promise to respect your authority and your wisdom as parents and to do my best to encourage your (son/daughter) to honor you as commanded by Scripture and to serve Christ at home as well as at church, at school, and in the world.

Signature: _____ Date: _____

PARENT RESOURCE LIBRARY

Many churches have libraries. Why not make sure yours is stocked with plenty of great resources for parents? If you can't purchase all the books you need, ask parents to buy books, read them, and then donate them to the library so other parents can borrow them and learn from them. There are hundreds of outstanding books on parenting and family issues that are available (I've written a few myself). Rather than providing a list of books and resources here (which would become outdated in time), I've posted a list of my "Top 20" parenting books on my Web site (www.waynerice.com). I'll also be happy to provide you with recommendations anytime if you e-mail me at wayne@waynerice.com.

While we're on the subject of books, try organizing a parents-of-teens book club. Buy a good parenting book for parents and have them read it together and discuss.

YOUTH CULTURE WATCH

Whenever you read an article, visit a Web site, or view a film that you think would be helpful to parents, pass it on to them by e-mail, publish it in your parent newsletter, post it on your Web site, put it in an event flyer (if it relates in some way), or do some combination of the above! We equip parents when we provide them with the knowledge they need to stay current on music, media, and other youth culture trends that are impacting their kids every day.

My friend Walt Mueller, of the Center for Parent/Youth Understanding, has developed a wonderful tool for evaluating and responding to popular culture that we can teach to parents as well as teens. He calls it his "3-d Guide" for making responsible choices about music and other media.[29]

★ **Discover:** What is it? What do you see? What do your hear? What is the message or worldview that's being presented? The first step is simply to observe.

★ **Discern:** How does it stand in light of what the Bible teaches or what I know to be truth? The second step is to evaluate what you see/hear as a Christian.

★ **Decide:** What do I do with this? What should my response be? Do I embrace it (I approve), should I ignore it (it's not important), or should I reject it (I'm opposed)? The final step is to take a course of action.

YOUTH CULTURE FIELD TRIPS

Go a step further: take a group of parents to a place where there are lots of teens (a mall or rock concert are two ideas for starters) and ask them to just observe. (Or ask them to do this individually.) Give them a list of questions: How are the teens dressed? How do they interact with each other? How many different kinds of teens can you spot? Anything about their behavior that reminds you of yourself when you were that age?

If you hold an event like this, take time afterward to debrief at a coffee shop or in someone's home. You can use the 3-d Guide above to discuss what you saw and heard.

PARENT MENTORS

Ask experienced parents in your church—or even grandparents!—to serve as mentors for parents of teens in your youth group. MOPS (Mothers of Preschoolers) does this quite effectively. If one-on-one mentoring seems awkward, ask parent mentors if they would be willing to host a dinner party once a quarter for other parents. Encourage them to build relationships with these parents and to make themselves available on an on-call basis.

ANSWERS CAFÉ

Parents have lots of questions about raising teenagers and plenty of other family issues. HomeWord has developed a terrific Internet resource called AnswersCafé. The great thing about it is you can make it part of your church or youth ministry Web site and add your own content; there are fees for this service. Check it out at www.homeword.com or www.answerscafe.com.

ACTION PLAN

★ Consider the questions under "Been There, Done That." If you're the parent of a child of *any* age, which of these questions are you most curious about? Are there questions you think should be added to this list? If you're not a parent, which of these questions seem most important to you? Least important?

MAKING IT WORK BY CONNECTING PARENTS

It's lonely being the parent of a teenager.

Not that you suddenly lose all your friends when your kids hit puberty (although that's possible!). It's more of a nagging feeling that you're the only parent in the world who doesn't have a clue.

When I conduct Understanding Your Teenager seminars, the most common response I get from parents is "It's just so good to know that I'm not alone." I've discovered that the vast majority of parents feel incredibly on their own and just need to know that what they're experiencing is normal.

One of the best gifts we can give to parents of teenagers is the gift of community. Parents of younger children seem to find it much easier to socialize and swap parenting ideas. But parents of teenagers are busier and less likely to share what's going on in their families.

The Bible says, "For lack of guidance a nation falls, but many advisors make victory sure" (Proverbs 11:14). So it is with parenting. When parents feel alone they are likely to feel embarrassed, guilty, ashamed, and hopeless, all of which can lead to defeat. That's why Christ gave us the church. The apostle Paul wrote in Galatians 6:2: "Carry each other's burdens." And that certainly applies to parents of teenagers.

If we can provide opportunities for parents to come together in a safe environment where they can share their hurts, worries, failures, and victories, they'll be encouraged and empowered, and they'll be much more likely to succeed with their kids at home. This chapter is about connections: parents getting help from each other, and parents connecting with their teens.

CONNECTING PARENTS WITH EACH OTHER
Parents of teenagers class

If your church has a regular Sunday school hour with breakout sessions for various age groups, why not have a class especially for parents of teenagers? Call it the ParenTeen Class or, for fun: Going to POT (POT, of course, stands for Parents of Teenagers). But any good name will do.

Ideally, this class should be led by an older adult, someone who has the gift of teaching and who also has some experience as a parent of a teenager. This could be someone from the church or youth ministry staff or one of the parents themselves.

The primary goal of the class is simply to connect parents of teenagers with each other. Like most Bible study groups and Sunday school classes, a parents-of-teens group can serve an important social function in the church as people get to know each other in a more intimate setting. Parents of teens are usually in the same age demographic and have a lot more in common than just the age of their kids.

The class can also serve as an unofficial support group for parents—though you probably won't want to call it that. As parents get to know each other they will, in fact, become a source of support for each other in a natural way. During class times parents can and will pray for each other and each other's families as needs are shared and requests made known.

The curriculum for the class can be nearly anything at all—it doesn't have to be about parenting teenagers. In fact, most people who attend Sunday school are likely to be more interested in going deeper into God's

Word and learning how to grow in their walk with Christ than talking about teenagers and parenting all the time. If you make every class a parenting seminar, you'll probably find that many parents stop attending.

On the other hand, you can invite guest speakers (like a family counselor or youth expert) or perhaps do an occasional six-week session on a parenting topic like "How to Help Your Teenager Grow Spiritually." Most parents are very receptive to getting some practical help on relevant topics from time to time.

The class also can be a great connection point for the youth ministry. One of your youth ministry staff (or one of the parents) can make an announcement each week updating them on youth ministry events, activities, prayer requests, and more.

If your church doesn't have a regular Sunday school hour, perhaps you can organize a class like this that meets at the same time your youth group meets, whether that's on Sunday or some other day or night of the week. This opens up the possibility of having joint sessions when parents and teens can meet together.

If your church has a small group ministry like mine does, you might encourage parents of teenagers to choose a small group that connects them with other parents of teenagers. Small groups are a big thing for most churches these days and most everyone in the church is encouraged to join one. People generally choose their group based on location, demographics, special interests, or topics. Create a small group or two for parents of teenagers and you'll likely get a good response.

TRUTH FROM THE TRENCHES

Small groups are a big thing for most churches these days. Create a small group or two for parents of teenagers and you'll likely get a good response.

Parent portraits

If you have a youth ministry newsletter, Web site, or bulletin board, collect family portraits from each family in your youth ministry and do a family profile each week (or as often as you can). Provide information on all the family members, along with interesting facts about each family like "favorite family tradition" or "favorite family vacation." This will help parents get to know each other better.

Family dinners

Do you have the gift of hospitality? If you enjoy having people to your home for dinner, consider inviting two or three couples (parents of teens in your youth ministry) that you think might enjoy meeting each other. Eat together, play a fun game or two, and focus the conversation on getting to know each other rather than letting it turn into a discussion of the youth ministry program.

POT parties

You may not want to call it a POT (Parents of Teenagers) Party (unless you want to get fired), but you can still throw an occasional party for the parents of your teens. Serve up some refreshments, play some fun games like How Well Do You Know Your Teenager? (I'll have more ideas for this game later in this chapter), and give parents time to socialize and get to know each other. If the gathering is large enough that you use nametags, have parents write their kids' names on the tag in addition to their own.

Parent idea sharing

Invite parents to share ideas with each other in your parent newsletter: "What I've done right" or "What I've learned from being the parent of a teenager" are starter ideas.

CONNECTING PARENTS WITH THEIR TEENS
Parent panels

One of the best ways to help parents share their faith and values with their own children is to invite them to be part of a parent panel at one of your youth group meetings. When my own children were teens, I always felt I had a slight advantage as a parent because I could preach and teach in front of the youth group and teach my kids at the same time (without mentioning their names, of course). We can give other parents the same opportunity by scheduling parent panels on a regular basis.

The basic idea is to bring in four or five parents to serve on a "panel of experts" on which they can either field questions from the audience or a moderator. There may be times when the topic itself will suggest the parents you want to invite. For example, if the panel topic is on serving God in the workplace, you can invite professionals from a variety of occupations. If the topic is drug abuse, you can invite parents who have had some experience with addicts, were once addicted themselves, or who work in the medical profession or in social services.

But you don't always need a topic to have a good panel discussion featuring parents. Here's a simple idea that works great: have your students write random questions on any topic and allow parents to answer them. If you can prepare your list of questions ahead of time, let the panelists prepare their answers in advance. You can even send the questions to parents who are unable to serve on your panel and read their answers along with the answers provided by panelists. Not all parents will feel comfortable in this type of setting, but it's a great way for students to get better acquainted with parents and to facilitate some intergenerational dialogue.

Teen panels

It probably goes without saying, but you can reverse the process above. If you do have a Parents of Teenagers Sunday morning class as I described earlier, a "panel of teen experts" can make an appearance at those classes and field questions from parents. This is a great way for parents to learn some things about the world of teenagers (and their own kids)!

Breakfast club

When my children were teens, I frequently took them out for breakfast as a way of catching up on what was going on in their lives. After sharing the idea at an Understanding Your Teenager seminar a few years ago, the youth ministry of the host church organized a breakfast club to encourage dads and their teens to do the same thing. Dads and teens joined the club simply by pledging to meet together one-on-one every week during the school year at the time and place of their choosing. At the end of the year all the members of the club gathered for a celebratory breakfast where they shared their experiences during the year.

This idea—or variations similar to it—can be implemented by either the youth ministry, the men's ministry, or the family ministry. Membership cards can be provided as well as other materials (such as a devotional booklet or discussion guide) to help dads and their teens get the most out of their time together. But the key is simply to promote this club well and to continue to urge parents and their teens to spend quality time together whenever they can, even if it's not at breakfast!

Letter writing

A great way to encourage good communication between teens and their parents is to provide them with opportunities to write letters to each other—the kind that involve actual paper and ink.

If your youth group members are going away to a camp, retreat, or other weekend experience where they'll be challenged spiritually, ask parents to write letters of encouragement to their teens ahead of time and to be praying for them while they're away. These letters can then be distributed to the students at an appropriate time during the trip when they can be read privately. They will have a powerful impact.

When you're teaching on a particular subject in your youth group meetings, why not ask parents to write a short letter to their teenager that focuses on that subject? Give them the Scripture verses you'll be covering or the main points of your lesson so they can reinforce or share their views on what you're teaching. Give them other guidelines and prompts to encourage their teens and to express some of what is on their hearts. Some examples might be:

★   What did they learn from their own experiences growing up?
★   What is their hope and prayer for their son/daughter?
★   What can they say to be an encouragement to him/her?

Remember that the key is to plan well in advance so parents will have time to write their letters and you'll have time to collect them for the event or meeting.

What if you can't get all the parents to write letters? As mentioned earlier in this book, don't let those parents set the agenda for the entire group. Do it anyway—take what you can get. For those students who might feel left out, you can always provide letters of encouragement from some of your adult leaders. Just remember—plan ahead. Almost all parents will participate if they have enough time to do it and if they don't feel pressured to write something they don't know anything about. Just make sure that they know their letter can be as simple as these few words: "I just want you to know that I love you and I am praying for you."

TRUTH FROM THE TRENCHES

Don't let those parents who don't want to join an activity set the agenda for the entire group. Work your plan anyway—take what you can get.

Teens also can write letters to their parents, of course. Just as with parents, give them some guidelines and prompts. Encourage your teens to keep their letters positive and to remember the Fifth Commandment—to honor their parents with their words. Suggest that they share with their parents what they're learning, what they're feeling, and any commitments they're making. You can collect the letters and mail them to the parents—or you can simply encourage your students to deliver their letters to their parents themselves. I still have fond memories of getting notes from my daughter, which she secretly slipped inside my briefcase before leaving for school in the morning. Those notes made my day—every time.

Parent-teen retreats

A camp or retreat for parents and teens (or entire families) can be a great way to give parents and their kids some quality time together to have fun and grow closer as a family. You can schedule it for one day, two days, a weekend, or a whole week. It could be held at a Christian conference center, a hotel, a campground (using tents and RVs), or even at the church. The possibilities are as endless as the benefits.

Parent-teen or family retreats don't necessarily need a full program or one that deals with family or parent-teen issues, although there are times when that may be appropriate. Most families just need some extended stress-free time to be together in a positive environment. If you can schedule in some time for parents and their children to have fun together by playing games, having devotions together, praying together, worshiping together, learning family communication skills together, and just growing spiritually together, so much the better.

Remember that parent-teen camps and retreats will require some serious advance planning. If you need some help, do your homework and check out some of the excellent resources that are available from resource providers like Youth Specialties, Group Publishing, and Standard Publishing's *One Girl Leader's Guide*.

Parent-teen mission and service projects

According to researchers, family acts of service rank as one of the primary ways parents pass their faith on to their kids.[30] If you plan mission trips and service projects for your students (which hopefully you do!), open them up to parents as well. Most mission trips require a fair amount of adult supervision and leadership anyway, so involve parents with their teens whenever you can.

Family mission trips are becoming more popular these days because many parents are looking for ways to do something more meaningful with their family vacation time than going to amusement parks and spending money on themselves and their kids. They know that one of the best ways to teach their children the values of the Christian faith is not by lecturing, but by example and experience. We can take advantage of this by encouraging parents and families to go on a short-term mission project where they can build houses for the poor, assist in a medical clinic, teach Vacation Bible School, or do disaster relief. With a little research you can find plenty of opportunities for families to serve together in nursing homes, homeless shelters, rescue missions, or ministries of the church. When parents and teens work side by side in ministry, good things invariably happen!

TRUTH FROM THE TRENCHES

Family acts of service rank as one of the primary ways parents pass their faith on to their kids. If you plan mission trips and service projects for your students, open them up to parents as well. Most mission trips need a fair amount of supervision and leadership anyway.

Stay-at-home week

This one will require some cooperation from the adult ministries of the church, but it's worth running up the flagpole to see if anybody salutes. The basic idea is to plan a week when all meetings are canceled and families are encouraged to do something together each night of that week (besides watching TV or doing homework). They can play games, watch family videos, work on a family service or craft project, clean the garage—it doesn't matter as long as they do it *together*, as a family. Families should also be encouraged to read Scripture and pray together each evening. You can provide resources like a family devotional booklet or DVD with a short message from the pastor to help facilitate this week.

Parent swap

Here's a crazy activity that can be fun and get families involved in the youth ministry at the same time. Have kids sign up for a "parent swap"—that is, they'll go live in someone else's house for twenty-four hours. This can quickly build relationships with parents and other teens in the youth group besides those in their own family. Teens living in each other's houses for a day or a weekend? Good way to find out how other families live.

A variation: have a family night event and ask teens to sit at tables with parents other than their own (this would also be great for the students whose parents don't normally attend). Give them questions to ask each other or play a table game that gets everybody acquainted with each other.

Parent-teen talk starters

Many parents have a tough time initiating conversations with their children about faith and values at home because (a) they don't know what to talk about and (b) they don't know how to do it without lecturing and nagging.

We can help by providing parents and teens with talk starters like the one below. Just put together a questionnaire on any topic and ask both the parents and their teens to answer the questions and compare their answers. A twist on this would be to have parents and teens try to guess each other's answers.

Encourage both the parents and the teens to answer all the questions as honestly as they can and to talk about them together without getting into an argument or shouting. Parents, especially, should be coached ahead of time to resist using their position as parents to scold or shame their children because they disagree with Mom or Dad. Someone once said that authority is like a bar of soap: the more you use it, the less you have. When parents learn to listen to their kids and have discussions rather than lectures, they'll have more authority, not less.

Here's an example of a good talk starter, with five questions, on the topic of church:

Question #1: How often should a person go to church?

- ❏ once a week
- ❏ once a year
- ❏ whenever he or she feels like it
- ❏ as much as possible
- ❏ other answers?

Question #2: Agree or disagree with these statements?

- ❏ Church is very important to me.
- ❏ I feel like I'm an important part of our church.
- ❏ The purpose of the church is to give the pastor something to do on Sundays.
- ❏ If church is boring, you should change churches.
- ❏ Families should sit together in church.
- ❏ Our church needs to change with the times.
- ❏ The youth ministry of our church is doing a good job.
- ❏ Add others of your own to this list!

Question #3: The main reason I attend church is . . . (choose three)

    ❏ To worship God
    ❏ To hear a good sermon
    ❏ To be with my friends
    ❏ It's a family tradition
    ❏ To grow spiritually
    ❏ I have responsibilities there
    ❏ To set a good example
    ❏ I would feel guilty if I didn't
    ❏ The Bible says we should go
    ❏ I like the music

Question #4: On a scale of one to ten (one = terrible, ten = fantastic), rate your church experience right now: ____. Talk about why you scored this the way you did.

Question #5: Read Hebrews 10:19-25 together. How do these verses apply to us today?

Sermon talk starters

If your students attend the church worship service with their parents (hopefully they do), encourage the teens to discuss the sermon—or the service in general—with their parents later that day. To facilitate this, ask the senior pastor (or whoever is preaching) to provide you with sermon notes or key questions to get the discussion rolling. Perhaps the questions can be printed each week in the church bulletin.

How well do you know your teenager?

Here's a simple game you can use to motivate discussion between parents and teens. First, have the teens answer each of the twenty questions below (or substitute/add other questions of your own). Then have parents go through the same list answering as they think their teen answered. See how many right answers the parents get. You also can do this in reverse—play the How Well Do You Know Your Parents? game—by changing the questions appropriately.

1. Your favorite TV show:
2. Your favorite class at school:
3. Your favorite teacher:
4. Your favorite food:
5. Your best friend's name:
6. Your best friend's parents' names (their mom and/or dad):
7. Your favorite band (or recording artist):
8. Your favorite Web site:
9. Your favorite hobby or pastime:
10. The last book you read:
11. The last movie you went to see at the theatre:
12. Where you would like to go on vacation:
13. What you would like to do as a career:
14. Your favorite sport:
15. Your favorite sports team:
16. Your favorite celebrity:
17. Your most prized possession:
18. The biggest influence in your life (person):
19. Your favorite Bible verse:
20. Your favorite Bible story:

Scoring:

18-20 correct—Congratulations! You and your teenager are very close!

15-17 correct—Not too bad, but a little more time with your teen couldn't hurt anything.

12-14 correct—Hmmm . . . apparently you've not been paying attention!

11 or less correct—Spend some time getting acquainted with your teenager!

Of course, many parents will be surprised by how many they didn't get correct. Encourage them to sit down with their teens and talk about each item on the list. Doing this can provide some great discussion and really help parents and teens get to know each other better.

Parent Q&A

To encourage conversations between parents and teens give students a Question of the Week for their parents to answer. Print the question on cards and have your students take them home, get their parents to answer the question, and then turn them in each week with their parents' answers to qualify for a prize drawing. After you announce the winner, ask some of the students to share what they learned from their parents, or read to the group some of the answers (anonymously, unless both parents and teens give you permission).

The questions you ask can be tied in with the curriculum or teaching that you're doing with your students, or they can be random ones like:

- ★ When you were my age, who was your biggest hero?
- ★ When you were my age, what was your biggest temptation?
- ★ What day in your life would you like to live over?
- ★ What's the best advice your mom or dad ever gave you?
- ★ Do you think growing up was harder when you were a teenager? Or now?
- ★ Do you think church attendance is necessary in order to be a Christian?
- ★ . . . And come up with plenty more!

Parent-teen game nights

Busy parents sometimes just don't have, or make, enough time to spend with their kids. So why not plan ahead and schedule an occasional parent-teen game night? You can play *Family Feud*-type games, board games, or indoor and outdoor games of all kinds. There are literally thousands of youth group games that can be played with parents. Some can be adapted to facilitate parent-teen teamwork. Here's a crazy one: try playing volleyball with parents and their teens tied together at the wrists. It's hilarious and a lot of fun. You can also have some parents-against-the-teens games or even hold entire tournaments pitting teens against their parents.

Chip off the old block

Collect pictures of the parents of the students in your youth group . . . when *they* were teens. Project them on the big screen next to pictures of their teen. Have your teens vote on who looks most like their parents. Do it just for fun or use it to kick off a discussion on family values, influences, what we learn from our parents, and more.

ACTION PLAN

★ Knowing your youth group and its dynamics, what are the best ways you can connect parents to parents? What about parents to their teens?

MAKING IT WORK BY INVOLVING PARENTS

Dale and Toni Smith are parents who have served as adult volunteers with the youth ministry at Shadow Mountain Community Church (El Cajon, California) for more than two decades. When I watch them interact with our middle schoolers every week, it's easy to see why the kids love them so much. Dale once told me, "We started working with The Crew (the middle school ministry) years ago when our daughter Nikki was in the group and later when our son Jake became a middle schooler. We also worked with the high school ministry for a couple of years but God gave us a real love for junior highers. We've been working with them ever since and we just love being able to help young people come to know and serve Jesus at this crucial time of life. It just breaks our hearts that more parents don't get involved."

Dale and Toni are prime examples of the great things that can happen when parents get involved in the youth ministry of the church. As a couple, they've provided stability and maturity to a youth ministry that has seen dozens of younger college students, young adult interns, and youth pastors come and go. They've been mentors and role models for hundreds of young teens over the years, including their own.

Dale and Toni are heroes of mine. So are thousands of other parents I've met through the years who have served in some way as youth leaders and volunteers. Despite the common stereotype of parents who are too busy, too old, too unpopular, or too set in their ways, parents can and should be involved in the youth ministry of their church.

In truth, every parent whose child is part of your youth ministry is already involved whether he or she realizes it or not. They are either reinforcing what their kids are learning and experiencing—or they're undermining it. Parents are hardly ever neutral. Your goal should be to help parents maximize their influence and to take advantage of the key role they play in the lives of their kids.

TRUTH FROM THE TRENCHES

Every parent whose child is part of your youth ministry is involved in your ministry whether he or she realizes it or not. They are either reinforcing what their kids are learning and experiencing—or they're undermining it.

WHY PARENTS SHOULD GET MORE INVOLVED

Hopefully, this book has made a strong case for getting parents involved in youth ministry. But it's worth noting early in this final chapter a few good reasons—some new, some repeated from earlier in this book—why you shouldn't hesitate to invite parents to take an active role in your ministry:

★ Parents who are involved with the youth ministry will not only be better positioned to be spiritual leaders at home, they'll also have the opportunity to be mentors and friends to other people's kids.

★ The more parents get to know other people's kids, the more likely they'll be able to understand and relate to their own kids. (Without any doubt, my experience in youth ministry gave me a tremendous advantage as a parent.)

★ Parents bring to the table assets that younger leaders don't have (see chapter two). Among them: wisdom that can only come with age.

★ Parents who are involved in the youth ministry have more time with their own kids. The youth group can be a positive, shared experience for parents and teens together. Many teens never get that kind of experience with their parents—times of laughter, ministry, and spiritual growth.

★ Parents have a vested interest in the quality of the youth ministry by the very fact that their kids are part of it. While this can also be a negative (if they are overly demanding or impatient), the positive side is that parents will often work harder in the youth ministry and are more likely to contribute financially or in other ways to help you achieve success.

★ Parents have more maturity and stability than young, inexperienced leaders who are more prone to making mistakes. Mistakes like quitting the ministry too quickly, getting involved in inappropriate relationships, or simply making dumb decisions.

★ Parents can be advocates for you with other adults in the church, most notably those in leadership. I've had parent youth leaders who also served on the church's board of elders or served on a finance committee. That's not a bad person to have on your team.

★ Parents generally have automatic access to schools. It's tough for youth workers to get on a campus, but it's easy for a parent.

★ Parents have natural contact with students because their house is usually full of them.

★ Parents have credibility with other parents. If you've had a hard time getting some parents to respond to you, get another parent to make the call instead. Parents will listen to other parents.

HOW TO GET THEM INVOLVED

There are many ways for parents to get involved in youth ministry. They don't have to show up twice a week for youth group meetings, teach Bible lessons, or host a pizza party. Here are four levels of involvement that almost any parent can choose from.

Level one: Parents Who Care

It should be one of our primary youth ministry goals to enlist and engage every parent of every student to be involved as Parents Who Care. Even if parents can't volunteer to directly help with any youth group activities or functions, we can ask every parent to pray for the ministry, to provide feedback and advice on occasion, and to support and reinforce the mission of the youth ministry in their home. This is the kind of caring that goes beyond just dropping kids off and hoping for the best.

Enlisting parents as prayer partners is a great way to get parents involved on this level. (And keep in mind that you can also enlist other adults in the church to become prayer partners. Senior adults especially have more time to pray and they'll do so if they're asked and given specific things to pray for.)

Encourage prayer partners to pray for one or more of the students in the youth group on a regular basis. Parents will be praying for their own kids but give them somebody else's teens to pray for as well. Give your prayer partners photos and information about the other teens they are praying for. You can set this up as a "secret pal" kind of thing and encourage prayer partners to remember their kids on special days like birthdays and other special occasions. Maybe at the end of the year you can arrange for all your prayer partners and teens to gather together to reveal who was praying for whom.

Another good way to support and encourage your prayer partners is publishing or e-mailing a monthly (or weekly) prayer list, like the one below, or a prayer calendar with names of students to pray for on each day of the week. Parents will especially appreciate knowing that their own children are being prayed for on a regular basis. Other prayer requests also can be included in your e-mails.

Some parents will be willing to participate in a "prayer huddle" before each youth group meeting. Rather than simply dropping off their kids each week, these parents can meet with other parents and the youth staff for a short time of prayer. Something like this can have a powerful impact on both the ministry and the teens who observe that their parents care in this special and visible way.

Parents Who Care also can serve on parent advisory councils or occasional committees designed to provide you with feedback and advice. There's a deep well of experience and wisdom in parents who are willing to be involved in this significant way. It's up to us to take advantage of it.

Parents Who Care Prayer List

Please pray for . . .

★   The adult youth leaders:
  - Pray that they live godly, exemplary lives (see 1 Timothy 3:1-13).
  - Pray that they have the right words to say when they are preaching and teaching.
  - Pray that they get the help and resources they need to avoid burnout or discouragement.

★   The students:
  - Pray that they come to know Christ and serve him every day.
  - Pray that they always feel accepted, affirmed, and loved by other members of the group.
  - Pray that they find godly friends and mentors.
  - Pray that they have the courage to live out their faith every day at home, at school, and with friends.

★   The youth ministry:
  - Pray for protection during times of travel, for safety in general, and for good health during every youth group activity.
  - Pray for community—that the group members bond with each other and with the church as a whole.
  - Pray that every youth ministry meeting or activity will be fruitful and God-honoring.
  - Pray that the group will grow not just in numbers but also in its love for Jesus.

TRUTH FROM THE TRENCHES

There's a deep well of experience and wisdom in parents who are willing to be involved in your ministry on a Parents Who Care level. It's up to you to take advantage of it.

Level two: Parents Who Come

Parents Who Come are parents who are simply willing to come and hang out with the youth group on an occasional basis. As I wrote earlier, it's good to communicate an open-door policy to all parents; this lets them know that nothing is hidden and that they're always welcome to attend youth ministry meetings and activities. They don't have to do anything; their *presence* is all that's requested. (Just as with Parents Who Care, this policy can be extended to all adults in the church, not just parents.)

Some youth workers object to the open-door policy by arguing that (a) teenagers don't want their parents around, and (b) parents will inhibit teenagers from being open and honest in discussions and other times of sharing. There's some validity, on some level, with some teens, to both of these objections—but they're not insurmountable. They shouldn't stop us from bringing parents and teens together in positive ways.

Remember: it's a myth that teens don't want their parents around. I know there's plenty of "evidence" to the contrary (just read any teen blog), but the research and the kids themselves (when they are being honest) are more convincing. While teens have a serious love/hate relationship going on with their parents and have difficulty reconciling their need for autonomy with their need for parental love and affirmation, down deep they want a better, closer relationship with those same parents.

We all know there are times when kids need privacy and safe places to share what's in their hearts and minds. Encouraging parents to attend youth group activities doesn't necessarily exclude or eliminate those times and places. When it's appropriate to have teen-only times and parent-only times, you can still have them.

Let me also recommend that when you invite parents to come to youth group meetings and activities, give them some guidelines to make their experiences positive ones. Encourage parents to: spread out and mingle with the teens (engage in conversations, ask questions); be positive and affirming (don't criticize or scold); remember that they aren't there to enforce rules or spy on their own kids. Have them try sitting with some teens who aren't their kids (unless their teens invite them to join their group). Tell them to have fun and enjoy what's going on (even if it gets them out of their comfort zones)!

TRUTH FROM THE TRENCHES

While teens have a serious love/hate relationship going on with their parents, down deep they want a better, closer relationship with them. Parents Who Come can make simple but worthwhile investments in that relational growth.

Level three: Parents Who Contribute

Some parents are willing to do more than just come and hang out. They can help meet specific needs on a limited or occasional basis. They can help stuff envelopes, help write (or design) the newsletter, chair a parent advisory group, host a barbecue, or organize a fund-raiser. They can cook meals, drive the bus, lead a small group, go on a mission trip, loan a van, or give some money. They may be able to teach or speak to the youth group—or play the banjo (who knew?). Parents often have all kinds of unique or hidden talents, expertise, or experience you can put to good use in youth ministry.

Parents, of course, need to be asked to contribute; they rarely just volunteer. Sometimes we're reluctant to ask because we don't like rejection. Or we'd rather do it ourselves or hire someone else to do it. But parents are usually willing and happy to help if they can. Remember that when a parent says no, they aren't saying no forever. Find out what their no means and, unless they want to be removed from your Parents Who Contribute list, keep giving them more opportunities to be involved. If nothing else, your regular phone call is a good way to stay in touch and keep the communication lines open.

Remember to invite parents to contribute well in advance of when you need them. Don't call parents and ask for help a day or two before (or worse, the day of) an event. This makes you look unorganized and unprofessional. Instead, plan ahead and give parents time to think about it, pray about it, and let you know by a date you give them. You'll get a much higher response that way.

To save yourselves, and the parents, a lot of unnecessary calls, perhaps at the start of the year (when you do a parent survey) you can ask parents to answer a questionnaire like the one that follows. It will give you a head start in putting together your Parents Who Contribute team.

We'd Love Your Help!

Would you be willing to help out with our youth ministry, even if it's on a limited basis? Let us know how!

How much time would you be willing to give?

_____ hours per (week/month/year)

Which of the following are ways that you can help?

❏ I can pray.

❏ I can lead a small group.

❏ I can go on a mission trip.

❏ I can do office work.

❏ I can lead games.

❏ I can lead worship.

❏ I can do graphic design.

❏ I can give my testimony.

❏ I can be a mentor to a youth who needs one.

❏ I can lead a parents group.

❏ I can cook or prepare snacks/refreshments.

❏ I can teach or preach.

❏ I can serve on an advisory committee.

❏ I can be a van driver.

❏ I can write articles for a parent newsletter.

❏ I can provide computer tech support.

❏ I can provide my home for meetings or social events (up to _____ kids).

❏ I can help with fund-raisers.

❏ I can be a camp counselor.

❏ I can lead a ministry team (drama, worship, computer/tech, missions, outreach, etc.).

❏ I would be willing to loan (or donate) my:

❏ car/van/pickup

❏ sports equipment

❏ computer

❏ video games

❏ ski boat

❏ motor home

❏ camcorder

❏ barbecue pit

❏ camping gear

❏ swimming pool

❏ other: ....
....
....
....
....
....
....
....
....
....
....
....
....
....
....
....

TRUTH FROM THE TRENCHES

Parents need to be asked to contribute; they rarely just volunteer. Sometimes we're reluctant to ask because we don't like rejection. Or we'd rather do it ourselves. But parents are usually willing and happy to help on a Parents Who Contribute level if they can.

Level four: Parents Who Commit

Every youth ministry requires a committed group of adult volunteers. These are the people who are there every week planning the programs, teaching the classes, leading the small groups, and building relationships with the teens. Obviously, a fair amount of time and energy is required, as well as a real sense of calling to youth ministry. It's not for the faint of heart.

That's why most youth workers today tend to be on the young side—often college students or young singles who aren't that far removed from adolescence themselves. There's nothing at all wrong with having young adults involved in the youth ministry. But Parents Who Commit can add some maturity, stability, and life experience to the student ministry leadership team that young adults alone can't provide. Involvement on this level also allows parents to become more actively involved in the spiritual training of their kids. As Dale and Toni told me, "When we lay our heads down on the pillow every night, we sleep well knowing that we were there for our kids. It has been such a blessing to us and to our family to be able to be actively involved in the youth ministry while our kids were teenagers."

Not all parents should be involved on this level, of course. They may not have the understanding, patience, personality, or relational skills needed to connect with teens. They may not have the time or their own kids may be uncomfortable with them serving as their youth leaders. These are all valid reasons for excusing them from serving on your leadership team. (But all parents can be involved on some level in a way that is appropriate for them.)

Parents who agree to serve on your leadership team will need to be interviewed, screened, trained, and commissioned just like any other adult volunteer in the youth ministry. When parents know that you're being careful about their involvement, it actually assures them that you're being just as careful about everyone else who is involved in the ministry. Marv Penner's book *Building & Mobilizing Teams*, which is part of this series, provides plenty of wisdom on how to put together a top-notch team of volunteers.

TRUTH FROM THE TRENCHES

Parents who agree to serve on your leadership team—Parents Who Commit—will need to be interviewed, screened, trained, and commissioned just like any other adult volunteer in the youth ministry. This actually provides those parents with a great deal of assurance.

Involving parents in youth ministry is not going to be without its problems, of course. But if you really care about helping parents win at home with their kids, the payoffs are huge. All of this will take time, patience, and a lot of hard work. The closer your youth ministry gets to a true partnership with parents, the more confidence and freedom you'll have in your calling to make disciples of teenagers. Engaging parents as allies in your youth ministry has tremendous benefits for both youth workers and parents, but the real winners are the teens.

ACTION PLAN

★ Do you have a vision for specific parents of teens in your ministry who could serve as Parents Who Care, Parents Who Come, Parents Who Contribute, or Parents Who Commit?

MAKING IT WORK: ENGAGING PARENTS AS ALLIES

★ How many parents of teens in your youth group do you know personally? List their names here and remember to pray for them regularly.

★ The Bible teaches children to honor and obey their parents. How do you reinforce that message in your students? How do you reinforce that even for teens whose parents may not be doing such a good job?

★ Who are some people you know who could share their knowledge and experience with parents of teenagers in your church?

★ Who do you think would benefit most from a family mission trip? The parents? The students? The youth leaders? The people who are being served on the trip? Share your reasons.

★ Any parent can become part of the church's youth ministry leadership team. Agree or disagree?

About Wayne Rice (Wayne's World)

Wayne Rice writes and speaks about teenagers to parents, youth workers, and anyone else who will listen. A veteran youth worker, he is the cofounder of Youth Specialties, an organization that has provided resources and training for youth workers for more than forty years.

Wayne has written more than twenty books for youth workers, parents, and teens, including *Junior High Ministry*, *There's a Teenager in My House*, and *Read This Book or You're Grounded*.

Over the past twenty years, he's presented his Understanding Your Teenager seminar to thousands of parents all over the world. Wayne also serves as a ministry consultant for churches and other organizations that want to better equip and encourage parents and families.

Wayne is married to Marci; they have three children and (so far) three grandchildren. Wayne also plays the banjo—quite well, actually. He's part of a bluegrass band, "Lighthouse."

For more information about Wayne's ministry, visit www.waynerice.com.

Notes

1. Mark DeVries, *Family-Based Youth Ministry: Revised and Expanded* (Downers Grove, IL: InterVarsity Press, 2004), p. 68.

2. "Most Twentysomethings Put Christianity on the Shelf Following Spiritually Active Teen Years," The Barna Group, September 11, 2006, www.barna.org/FlexPage.aspx?Page=BarnaUpdate&BarnaUpdateID=245 (accessed March 1, 2009). The most potent data regarding disengagement is that a majority of twentysomethings—61 percent of today's young adults—regularly attended church at one point during their teenage years but are no longer spiritually engaged.

3. "LifeWay Research Uncovers Reasons 18 to 22 Year Olds Drop Out of Church," LifeWay Staff, LifeWay: Biblical Solutions for Life, www.lifeway.com/lwc/article_main_page/0%2C1703%2CA%25253D165949%252526M%25253D200906%2C00.html (accessed February 27, 2009).

4. Christian Smith with Melinda Lundquist Denton, *Soul Searching: The Religious and Spiritual Lives of American Teenagers* (New York, NY: Oxford University Press, 2005), pp. 30-71. The Mormon Church—which neither employs professional clergy nor professional youth workers—has bucked this trend. Parents are charged with the religious and moral training of their children and given the tools to make it happen.

5. Tom Carpenter, "Busting the Drop Out Myth," *Group Magazine* (Loveland, CO; March-April 2007).

6. There's no way of knowing exactly how many youth workers there are, of course, but researchers at *Group Magazine* estimate that there are about sixty thousand full-time (paid) youth workers, twenty thousand part-time (paid) workers, and approximately two hundred thousand volunteers who are leading their church's youth ministries. *Group Magazine* (January-February 2009), p. 60.

7. Smith and Denton, *Soul Searching: The Religious and Spiritual Lives of American Teenagers*, p. 266.

8. Michael Cromartie, "What American Teenagers Believe: A Conversation with Christian Smith," *Books & Culture* (January-February 2005), pp. 10, 11.

9. "What You Said: What Parents Want Their Youth Leaders to Know," from HomeWord's "Good Advice" parent newsletter (San Juan Capistrano, CA: HomeWord, May 2007), www.homeword.com/Articles/ArticleDetail.aspx?iArticleId=597 (accessed March 16, 2009).

10. From a *Newsweek/USA Today* poll of 758 ten-to-seventeen-year-olds and their parents published in *Newsweek*, November 22, 1993, p. 53. Top influences were ranked as follows: parents, 86 percent; grandparents, 56 percent; place of worship, 55 percent; teachers, 50 percent; peers, 41 percent; community organizations, 23 percent; media, 22 percent.

11. Kevin Donovan, "Teenagers Choose Parents Over David Beckham," *Christianity Today*, January 23, 2007, www.christianitytoday.com/articledir/print.htm?id=9236 (accessed March 16, 2009).

12. Smith and Denton, *Soul Searching: The Religious and Spiritual Lives of American Teenagers*, p. 261.

13. Jay Kesler, *Raising Responsible Kids: Ten Things You Can Do Now to Prepare Your Child for a Lifetime of Independence* (Brentwood, TN: Wolgemuth & Hyatt, 1991), pp. 90, 91.

14. George Barna, *Revolutionary Parenting: What the Research Shows Really Works* (Carol Stream, IL: Tyndale House Publishers, 2007), pp. 11, 12.

15. Mark DeVries, "Getting (and Keeping) Parents On Your Team," *Group Magazine* (Loveland, CO, January 2, 2003), p. 48.

16. Kurt Johnston, *Middle School Ministry Made Simple* (Cincinnati, OH: Standard Publishing, 2008), p. 40.

17. *Incarnational* is a word we use to describe the ministry of "being with" teenagers. It is based on the Incarnation of Jesus Christ described in the first chapter of the Gospel of John. Just as "the Word became flesh and made his dwelling among us" (John 1:14), so we as youth workers (adults) can't do youth ministry from a distance but instead we temporarily leave our adulthood and "dwell among" students so that we can identify and communicate effectively with them.

18. Mark Holmen, *Building Faith at Home: Why Faith at Home Must Be Your Church's #1 Priority* (Ventura, CA: Regal Books, 2007).

19. DeVries, *Family-Based Youth Ministry: Revised and Expanded*, pp. 16, 17.

20. May I suggest Wayne Rice, ed., *There's a Teenager in My House*, featuring 101 questions parents ask about raising teenagers. The questions are answered by Marv Penner, Duffy Robbins, Mark DeVries, and other members of the Understanding Your Teenager seminar team (Downers Grove, IL: InterVarsity Press, 2008).

21. "Q & A with Doug Fields," *Group Magazine* (Loveland: CO, November-December 2008), p. 18.

22. There are a number of Web sites touting this movement, but one of the better ones is www.faithbeginsathome.com.

23. George Barna, *Transforming Children into Spiritual Champions: Why Children Should Be Your Church's #1 Priority* (Ventura, CA: Regal Books, 2003), p. 78.

24. For further reading on this topic, see Jack Crabtree, *Better Safe than Sued: Keeping Your Students and Ministry Alive* (Grand Rapids, MI: Zondervan/Youth Specialties, 2008).

25. "Blintzes and Sour Cream, Wherefore?: The Culinary Art of Shavuot," *Jewish Heritage Online Magazine*, http://jhom.com/calendar/sivan/dairy.htm (accessed March 10, 2009).

26. Marv Penner, *The Complete Youth Worker's Guide to Parent Ministry: A Practical Plan for Defusing Conflict and Gaining Allies* (Grand Rapids, MI; Zondervan/Youth Specialties, 2003), p. 22.

27. I've written a seminar presentation called "Rock the House" that accompanies *Read This Book or You're Grounded.* If you'd like a copy of the seminar notes, PowerPoint slides, or more, visit my Web site at www.waynerice.com for more information.

28. Merton Strommen and A. Irene Strommen, *Five Cries of Parents: New Help for Families on the Issues That Trouble Them Most* (New York, NY: Harper and Row, 1985).

29. Walt Mueller, *How to Use Your Head to Guard Your Heart: A 3-d Guide to Making Responsible Music Choices* (Elizabethtown, PA: The Center for Parent/Youth Understanding, originally published 2003), www.cpyu.org.

30. David and Kathy Lynn, *HomeGrown Faith: You Can Nurture Your Kids in the Christian Faith!* (Nashville, TN: World Publishing, 2006), p. 24.

Y★UTH MINISTRY IN THE TRENCHES

Engaging & Inspiring Youth Ministry Reading

Filled with practical ideas, these youth ministry books are "return-to" resources written in an easy-to-read style. Our featured authors—Marv Penner, Wayne Rice, and Rick Bundschuh—have more than a half-century of youth ministry experience in the trenches!

Reaching Unchurched Teens remains an area of confusion and difficulty—even anxiety—for many youth leaders who want to provide their students with practical tools for reaching their friends who don't know Christ.

Building & Mobilizing Teams is a critical need at a time when many leaders feel the need for more help, the necesity of delegating, and the importance of highly involved volunteers who care deeply for students.

Engaging Parents as Allies —making sure they're involved and feel needed—is critical as youth ministry continues to evolve. Many leaders are experiencing an increasing need to involve parents in ministry—not push them away.